I WISH I READ
THIS BOOK BEFORE
LAW SCHOOL

This book was conceived, designed, and produced by The Bright Press, an imprint of the Quarto Group, The Old Brewery, 6 Blundell Street, London N7 9BH, United Kingdom. T (0)20 7700 6700 www.QuartoKnows.com

All inquiries should be addressed to:
Peterson's Publishing, LLC
4380 S. Syracuse Street, Suite 200
Denver, CO 80237-2624
www.petersonsbooks.com

ISBN: 978-0-7689-4563-8

The Bright Press
Publisher: James Evans
Editorial Director: Isheeta Mustafi
Art Director: James Lawrence
Managing Editor: Jacqui Sayers
Development Editor: Abbie Sharman
Editor: Anna Southgate
Design: Lindsey Johns
Cover Design: Grade

Printed and bound in China

9 8 7 6 5 4 3 2 1

I WISH I READ THIS BOOK BEFORE LAW SCHOOL

ADVICE FROM TOP PROFESSORS ON HOW TO ADJUST, SUCCEED, AND THRIVE

JENDAYI SAADA, LESLIE P. CULVER, AND ROBIN APODACA

ABOUT THE AUTHORS

JENDAYI SAADA

Lead author Jendayi Saada is Associate Dean of Student & Faculty Development and Assistant Professor of Law at The University of La Verne College of Law. In her current position, she leads a team of dedicated, highly skilled faculty members that has developed a comprehensive academic and bar support program that spans new student orientation through bar passage and includes curriculum enhancements in all three years. If asked about the most gratifying aspect of her career in legal education, her answer is loud and clear, "Helping students achieve their dream of becoming a lawyer!"

LESLIE P. CULVER

Author of the legal writing, self-care, and diversity chapters, Leslie P. Culver is a Professor (Clinical) of Law at the University of Utah S.J. Quinney College of Law. She teaches legal methods and upper-level seminars related to cultural awareness and identity performance. She is also a professional consultant on topics related to diversity, equity, and inclusion.

ROBIN APODACA

Author of the career development chapters, Robin Apodaca is Director of Career Services at Chapman University, School of Law. She has over 16 years of law school career services experience. Her responsibilities include helping to develop and implement strategies for career advising, employer outreach, and programming services; advising law students and alumni; overseeing the 1L Professional Development program; and fostering and maintaining relationships with employers.

CONTENTS

INTRODUCTION

Greetings, future lawyer:

Wouldn't it be fantastic if you had all the answers BEFORE
you took the test? It is often said that hindsight is 20/20.
Looking back over our previous experiences, we can clearly
see all of the valuable information and lessons that lay
hidden from us at the time. From my position as a professor
and law school administrator, I look back at my own law
school experience and think how different it might have
been if I knew then what I know now! Usually, you have to
go through the experience to have hindsight, but *I Wish I
Read This Book Before Law School* gives you the advantage
of knowing the essentials before you even pack your bags.

Historically, law school and the legal profession were reserved for a small and select group of people, but our current and future societies demand a broader, more diverse practicing bar that reflects all of its members. As our societies change, so should the critical people who are primarily tasked with representing them and shaping the laws that govern them: lawyers. Regardless of your age, where you exist on the socioeconomic ladder, your race, gender, or national origin, your voice, life experiences, and aspirations for the future need to be represented in the next generation of legal advocates.

Every legal career begins in law school—from the legal knowledge and skills you develop, to your connections in the community, to building a solid reputation when you become a member of the practicing bar. It is a journey that only the bravest and most disciplined and skilled people complete. Typically, it is a time of trial and error, but this book can significantly reduce the number and gravity of the errors you make as you progress.

Going to law school is an endeavor worthy of your time, energy, and money. It will teach you more about yourself than you might have thought possible. Make the most of it by researching, planning, studying, learning, and growing through the process. The journey through law school may feel like an eternity at the beginning, but like all good marathons, the finish line is waiting, and with preparation and endurance, you will cross it. Then, it's on to the next race!

This is YOUR time! Make every minute and every experience count! After reading this book, you will know what to pack for your journey through law school. Your future awaits. Get ready to run!

Wishing you all the best!

ABOUT THIS BOOK

This book is a roadmap designed to help you begin your journey into the legal profession. The book is divided into four parts, and you can either start from the beginning and go straight through (recommended if just starting your law school journey) or skip around based on your current needs if your journey has already begun.

PART 1 of this book provides information that will help you make choices about which type of law school you should attend, how to create an impressive application package that makes you attractive to your chosen law school, and how to prepare for the journey ahead. It also propels you forward in time, giving you a glimpse of what you can expect in your final year, the licensing exam, and your legal career so that you can plan well in advance for success.

PART 2 is like a crystal ball that allows you to peer deeply into your first year of law school and see where the pitfalls lie so that you can easily step around them. In this section, you will learn how to navigate your courses, develop strong study habits, and create and maintain a positive mindset for learning.

Throughout the chapters are quotes from faculty and students with their key advice and a host of tips from professionals. At the end of the book, you'll find Resources with some templates for you to use or modify, as well as Further Reading with a recommended bibliography for additional publications on some of the subjects covered.

PART 3 provides insight into what you can expect for the remainder of your law school career and how to prepare for your career after law school is over. Understanding where you are going is critical to deciding how best to get there. Use Part 3 to guide your choices of doctrinal courses, experiential courses, and your licensing exam so that you can have the career you want and deserve.

PART 4 provides valuable information and tips for achieving the goals you set before coming to law school. How you arrive at your final destination is as important as getting there. Part 4 also provides you with tools for self-care so that you can avoid burnout and be healthy and happy during your journey through law school and beyond!

CHAPTER ONE

PREPARING FOR LAW SCHOOL

Consider law school as a process of becoming. The preparation for law school is only the warm-up lap in a three- to four-year marathon, but getting a good start will bring you that much closer to the finish line. Researching and planning your law school experience will help you make sure you are in the right race and the right place!

Law schools are as competitive as the students who fill their halls. There's a lot that goes into the decision about which law school will best meet your needs. Think of all of the things you would consider when planning the vacation of your dreams. "What's the weather like at that time of year?" "What kind of activities will you be able to do?" "Roughly how much will your trip cost?" Imagine picking a destination, arriving excited for your dream trip, just to find that the weather is miserable, there are no activities that excite you, and the trip was more expensive than you expected! Choose your law school as carefully as you would your dream vacation. Make the journey worth going!

This chapter provides important information and tips for beginning your legal career. Choosing the right law school and building an impressive application package are critical first steps. After you have been admitted, developing or sharpening learning skills and habits can improve your performance right from the start. If you are a nontraditional student, starting law school may require extra preparation, and this chapter looks at particular considerations for you. Using your time and resources wisely will pave a clear path for success throughout law school and beyond.

Get ready to run!

THE RIGHT SCHOOL

All law schools are not equal, so choosing the school that best fits your needs is the first step to a happy law school experience. Here are a few things to consider when choosing the right law school for you.

TYPE OF ACCREDITATION

The type of accreditation—whether national, regional, and/or state—matters, especially for employment opportunities and your ability to take a licensing (bar) exam in other jurisdictions. In the United States, graduates of law schools that are accredited by the American Bar Association (ABA) are able to sit for a bar exam in any state or U.S. territory. Other regions or countries will have their own requirements for accreditation and eligibility to practice law. See also, Chapter Seven: Taking the Bar Exam.

ADMISSION CRITERIA

You may be required to attain certain undergraduate grades, entrance or aptitude examination scores, and meet character and fitness requirements. While most law schools in the United States still require the Law School Admissions Test (LSAT), increasingly, U.S. law schools are accepting other standardized exams, such as the Graduate Record Examination (GRE), or do not require a test score at all. In many

other countries, including the United Kingdom, the undergraduate degree itself is the law degree. See also page 18: Admission Factors.

PART-TIME PROGRAMS

If you are planning to work during your studies, part-time programs offer a path to a legal education over an extended period of time. Full-time programs are usually designed to be completed in three years, while part-time programs may take four.

DUAL-DEGREE PROGRAMS

Some law schools offer dual-degree programs (for example, JD/MBA, JD/MPP) or concurrent programs that allow students to earn the law degree and another advanced degree simultaneously. These programs will enhance your legal degree and can give you an edge in your job search over other applicants who have only studied for the law degree. See also pages 56–59: Course Selection.

DO YOUR HOMEWORK

1 Check law school rankings

These may be published in a national magazine, periodical, or website for the agency responsible for national accreditation of law schools. Among the factors that count are entrance exam scores, bar exam pass rate, job placement rates, expenditure per student, student-to-faculty ratio, library resources, and median undergraduate grade point average. While rankings don't tell the complete story, they can inform you of a school's standing among its peers.

2 Visit the Law School Admission Council (LSAC) website

The LSAC is a virtual clearinghouse of information about the study of law. From the LSAT test to law school forums, and diversity issues in legal education to being the main portal for law school applications, this is a great resource, with links to almost all nationally accredited law school websites.

3 Read law school mission statements

Ideally, the school you choose to attend should be committed to a mission and set of values that are compatible with your own personal values. For example, some schools are steeped in specific religious philosophies, some are very conservative or liberal, others have a commitment to social justice and principles of diversity and inclusivity.

4 Talk to alumni

Seeking out and speaking with alumni is useful because they are often eager to share their personal experiences of the school as a whole, the student body, and the faculty/administration.

5 Talk to local employers

Local employers are often alumni of the schools that are resident in the same communities. Lawyers and judges attend school functions, form partnerships with law schools, provide intern- or externships to students, and hire their graduates. They have a unique perspective on the quality of education and training at a particular law school, as well as the level of access graduates of certain schools have to careers in the local community and beyond.

Use the template on page 200 to help compare the schools you consider.

AREAS OF CONCENTRATION

Some law schools offer legal concentrations specializing in particular areas of law, among them public interest, environmental law, business law, and international law. If you already have an idea of your desired area of practice, attending a law school with a concentration or specialization in that area can provide a deeper, richer experience in your chosen field. See also pages 56–57: Legal Concentrations.

TYPES OF CAREER OPPORTUNITIES

A law degree can lead to many career options, including judicial clerkships, government internships, and working for large firms or small local firms. This is definitely an area where your law school matters. Many coveted judicial clerkships highly favor students from top-tiered law schools. The same is true for jobs and internships at the more prestigious law firms. If your goal is to land one of these jobs, researching the selection process is key. See also Part 4: Career and Professional Development.

LICENSING AND EMPLOYMENT RATES

A license, or legal practice certification for the practice of law, goes hand in hand with employment rates. For example, in many countries including the United States, you cannot work as an attorney without passing a bar exam and meeting other licensing requirements. Many employers will not make advance job offers or even hire graduates from schools with persistently low bar pass rates. Check out the requirements for legal practice in the country in which you plan to operate.

REPUTATION IN THE LEGAL COMMUNITY

As is true for most universities and colleges, a law school's local community engagement is important. Many potential employers and firms that offer scholarships and internships partner with their local law school. The strength of these partnerships is important, especially if you plan to live and work locally after you graduate.

ALUMNI ENGAGEMENT

Alumni organizations offer terrific networking, mentoring, and hiring opportunities for students at their alma maters. An engaged alumnus is a bonus for you because its connections in the legal community may lead to job opportunities. See also Chapter Ten: Networking.

DIVERSITY AND INCLUSIVITY

Exposure to a diverse set of experiences and ideas is a critical component of legal education, as your eventual clients will likely come from varied backgrounds. Also, many students feel more comfortable learning from faculty and peers who share some collective experiences. Research what diversity and inclusivity among faculty, staff, and students actually looks like at your top law school picks. See also Chapter Sixteen: Diversity, Inclusion, and Equity.

Whatever your political, religious, or social leaning, attending a school that supports those values is helpful.

ADMISSION FACTORS

Getting into a good law school is a competitive process. The more prestigious the school, the harder it is to get in. Law schools consider several factors when assessing an applicant for admission.

COMMON FACTORS

★ The information on your application form

★ The score you received on a standardized test such as the Law School Admissions Test (LSAT) in the United States and the National Admissions Test for Law (LNAT) in the United Kingdom

★ Undergraduate transcripts indicating the completion of a required degree and your grades

★ Your personal/motivation statement

★ Letters of recommendation

★ Your work history

★ Your criminal background history

Each country and law school has its own set of requirements for admission. Always check a law school's admissions web page for their specific requirements. In addition to the requirements of your chosen law schools, it's always a good idea to check the jurisdictional requirements for licensing. Various countries and local jurisdictions may have particular requirements regarding personal and professional backgrounds of applicants that could be problematic for becoming licensed to practice. Specifically, a negative criminal history, allegations of academic dishonesty or disqualification from a previous educational institute, unresolved financial debt, and violations of court-ordered child support or alimony payments among other things, may delay or even prevent admission to the bar.

Pro tips

ENGLISH AS A SECOND LANGUAGE

If you speak English as a second language and are applying for a course taught in English, check whether your schools of choice require you to take an English language exam. Most U.S. schools will accept either the Test of English as a Foreign Language (TOEFL) or the International English Language Testing System (IELTS). Check the school's website for further information.

NONTRADITIONAL LAW STUDENTS

If you are not in your early 20s and fresh out of undergraduate school, chances are you're a nontraditional law student. This shouldn't deter you, but you should consider your strengths and weaknesses.

YOU MIGHT BE:

★ Working full-time
★ Changing careers
★ Returning to school after a long break
★ The first member of your family to go to law school
★ Caring for a child/children or a parent

In many cases, your work/life experience and/or your role as a parent or caregiver will mean that you are coming to law school with stronger time-management and problem-solving skills than your younger, greener cohorts. If you are a first-generation student, you probably won't find a more motivated, determined person in your class. If you are a working student or have children, you may need to attend law school part-time. Part-time programs generally take four years instead of three, and classes may be offered during the day or in the evenings. While you will take fewer classes each semester, the work is no less rigorous than a full-time program.

NEED INSPIRATION?

Inspirational stories about nontraditional students abound. One student completed law school at the age of seventy-two! He had retired from another profession and decided that now was the time to live his dream of becoming a lawyer! He graduated and passed the bar exam on his first try.

Another student was widowed with three young children. She had made her husband—a foreign diplomat from an African nation—a deathbed promise that she would live out the potential he saw in her and go to law school. She did just that and is now a practicing lawyer, with her two daughters having followed in her footsteps.

Key considerations

Is your partner on board? This is important because they may need to take on more responsibilities around the house and possibly increase their income to accommodate the time you spend on your studies.

Will you need childcare? If you are a single parent of young children, you will need to have a solid plan in place for childcare, especially around final exam periods.

Are you out of practice? Grammar and sentence structure are important features of legal writing. If it's been a while, you may need a refresher.

What will self-care look like for you? Between work, kids, spouse, school, and so on, you will need to plan time for you to rejuvenate so that you don't get burned out.

SHARPEN YOUR SKILLS

If you've ever told a lawyer or barrister that you plan to go to law school, their first response was likely, "Law school is hard. It's not like undergraduate school." The practice of law demands a particular skill set and critical thinking at the highest level so that you are fully equipped to be the best problem-solver and advocate for your clients.

Here is a list of skills and habits you will need from day one of law school and suggestions for developing them before you attend.

READING COMPREHENSION

Whatever country you are in, the law is developed in a historical, social, political, and economic context, so it is important to have at least a basic knowledge of these topics. Read lots of books and articles, especially on subjects that foster critical thought, such as philosophy.

SPEED-READING

The sheer volume of reading in law school can be daunting. You will need to read fast, yet still be able to grasp important concepts and nuances in the material. Practice speed-reading documents of all kinds for important information and a strong conceptual understanding.

"There is a vague popular belief that lawyers are necessarily dishonest. Let no young man choosing the law for a calling for a moment yield to the popular belief. Resolve to be honest at all events; and if in your judgment you cannot be an honest lawyer, resolve to be honest without being a lawyer."

Abraham Lincoln

ANALYTICAL WRITING

Work on your grammar, sentence and paragraph structures, and organization. A good basic grammar book or refresher course can strengthen your writing skills.

CRITICAL THINKING

Always question or challenge things that you read and hear for proof of accuracy or alternative perspectives.

TIME MANAGEMENT

Practice developing schedules and checklists for daily, weekly, and monthly tasks—and devise a range of strategies for sticking to them.

SELF-REGULATION

Legal education requires you to be a self-directed learner. Practice reflecting on, monitoring, self-assessing, and improving activities that you do on a daily basis.

These are skills that you will continue to develop throughout your studies. Consider them a warm-up for the marathon that awaits you in law school.

FINANCIAL PLANNING

Going to law school is a grand endeavor and the financial investment in your degree is no small matter either. Plan ahead for the expenses that come along with legal education.

EXTENDED BUDGET PLANNING

At the start of law school, it's a good idea to create an extended budget that will cover your entire legal education program. As you advance through each level of law school, other costs will arise. Creating a savings plan for these costs in advance will save you money and heartache later.

FEES ASSOCIATED WITH THE BAR EXAM

The requirements to become a licensed attorney after graduation are covered later in the book. For now, just know that there are hefty fees for the bar exam application, moral character applications, and fees for registering as a student with the state bar, among others. These combined fees, depending on where you plan to take the exam, can run close to US$2,000. See also Chapter Seven: Taking the Bar Exam.

POST-GRADUATION COSTS

Another significant cost of licensing is a post-graduation bar review course (see also, pages 90–91: Bar Review Courses). After the time and money spent attending law school, you don't want to become suddenly frugal when it comes to preparing for your bar exam. Most U.S. law school graduates purchase a commercial bar review program designed to help them prepare for the bar exam. These programs can cost from several hundred to several thousand dollars. Other countries may have additional or fewer fees for licensing. Budgeting in advance for these extra costs can save you from having to take out private loans with potentially high interest rates at the end of law school. See also pages 80–81: Your Finances.

TIME OFF WORK TO STUDY

Finally, most graduates choose not to work during the bar exam preparation period between graduation and the actual exam (eight to ten weeks in the United States). Having the time to focus on studying is one of the most important factors in successfully passing the exam on the first attempt. Begin your bar preparation savings plan from the first day of law school so that when you graduate you can ease into studying, without worrying about how you will pay your bills. See also page 82: Study Time.

Money matters

Below is a sample budget, and you can use the template on page 202 to create your own. You will need to factor in both anticipated and unanticipated costs. Check your preferred school's website for cost of attendance.

Expense	Year	Anticipated amount per year
Tuition	1–3	$50,000
Student fees	1–3	$800
Books and course materials	1–3	$1,400
Housing	1–3	$8,000
Food	1–3	$3,000
Health insurance plan (if not included in Student fees)	1–3	$1,200
Monthly bills (phone, utilities, transportation, etc.)	1–3	$3,000
Technology (hardware/software) and subscriptions	1–3	$100
Application and registration fees for exams, licensing, or certifications	3	$1,800
Bar exam review material	3	$2,500
Travel during breaks in school	1–3	$1,000
Professional clothing	1–3	$400
Total	**for three years**	**$211,000**

PART

YOUR FIRST YEAR

CHAPTER TWO

THE TYPICAL FIRST YEAR

The first year of law school is filled with necessary contradictions. You may very well find that you are both excited and terrified by the intellectual race you have entered. It is a year of tearing down old ways of thinking and writing and building up new ways as you learn the skills of lawyering. It is the year you will learn that "It depends!" is usually the right answer to the problem. Most of all, the first year is about navigating the newness of the law school journey.

Undergraduate programs offer a wide choice of areas in which to major or minor, so the first year of your program may include general, introductory level courses in such subjects as math, language, history, and so on. Law school is specifically focused on legal principles and practice, and most programs of legal education include the same or a similar set of foundational courses. However, don't be fooled by the introductory nature of the first-year courses. These courses are foundational, but they are not, by any degree, easy. The difficulty lies not only in learning the actual subject matter, but in the level of skill you will be expected to develop as you learn to read, write, and think like a lawyer!

This chapter describes the typical classes you will likely be required to take in your first year, including law courses, legal writing courses, and academic skills courses. Grade evaluation and ranking, and the process of learning to think like a lawyer are also discussed. There are tips for developing critical academic skills, managing your workload, and developing and maintaining a winning mindset. You will likely run harder and faster in your first year than you've ever run before. Just remember to pace yourself and you will make it to the finish line.

FIRST-YEAR COURSES

First-year law students generally take certain foundational courses depending on the country in which they are studying. While some U.S. law schools vary slightly in their first-year curriculum, most require students to take a standard set of courses. Legal education curriculums in other countries also tend to reflect the most fundamental principles and concepts of their legal systems. Whether these foundational courses are delivered over one semester or two depends on the school.

LAW COURSES

First-year law courses fall under the two most basic systems of law: the civil system and the criminal system. See the boxes below for key differences between them.

CONTRACT LAW (CIVIL)

This course covers the basic principles of contracting, including how contracts are formed; how to determine what terms are included; and how to interpret the terms, performance, breach, defences, remedies, and third-party relationships to the contract. Most of us form several contracts every day of our lives. Whether we are paying to park

at a parking meter, buying vegetables at the grocery store, or purchasing a movie ticket, the principles of contract law are at play.

TORT LAW (CIVIL)

Torts are "civil wrongs" for which the person who was wronged may receive some type of compensation. While contract law is based on agreements between the parties, tort law centers on a social contract, or how we, as a society, agree to interact as a whole. Tort law is based on the common law (developed from a line of previous legal cases) and/or statutory law (passed by a legislative body). You may already have experienced tort law in your personal life—

Civil system

* The most common penalty for a civil case is the payment of money or an injunction.

* Parties to a civil suit are plaintiffs and defendants.

Criminal system

* The penalty for a criminal case is typically a loss or potential loss of freedom.

* Parties are the "people" (state or federal government) and a defendant.

if you have ever been in a car accident, been bitten by a dog, or been shoved by a schoolyard bully, for example.

PROPERTY LAW (CIVIL)

First-year property law often covers personal property (things) and real property (land). If you have ever purchased or rented an apartment or house, you have experience of real property law. If you have ever lost, found, or misplaced an item, you have experienced personal property law. Property law, more than contracts or torts, employs a lot of old and specialist language. Make sure you purchase a legal dictionary so that these terms don't get lost in translation.

FEDERAL CIVIL PROCEDURE

Civil procedure is very different from contract, tort, and property law, but is related in an intricate way. Think of these courses as your cardiovascular, digestive, and neurological systems, and civil procedure as the musculoskeletal system that houses and provides mobility to these systems. Civil procedure explores the "process" or stages of a lawsuit, from the initial filing of a case through to appeal. It is the glue that holds civil cases together.

CRIMINAL LAW

Criminal law is often taught as a one-semester course in the first year of law school. You will learn about the underlying policy rationales of crime and punishment, as well as the various categories of crimes. If you are a lover of crime dramas, you will no doubt have seen the criminal justice system in play on television or in the movies. You may be surprised to learn just how different real-life criminal law is from what you see on TV!

LEGAL WRITING

Regardless of whether you practice civil or criminal law, or whether you are a litigator (and try cases in a court of law) or a transactional lawyer (and draft legal documents), all lawyers must be able to research and write analytically. Writing is arguably the most basic and fundamental skill required for lawyers—a lawyer who can't write is like a doctor who can't diagnose. See Chapter Three: Legal Research, Analysis, and Writing and Chapter Five: Legal Research and Writing Beyond the First Year.

ACADEMIC SKILLS

Many law schools have adopted academic support programs (ASPs) that include mandatory or optional courses in the first year of law school. These courses may have names such as "Introduction to the Legal Process" or "Academic Skills," but their common purpose is to help students develop the critical skills necessary to effectively learn the legal principles in various subjects. Topics covered in these skills courses may include case reading, case briefing, time management, course outlining, rule articulation, analysis, and exam-taking skills, to name a few. Whether you find learning and using the law incredibly difficult or relatively easy, ASP courses can help you develop an edge, to keep your edge, or to expand it.

MAKING THE GRADE

Like many aspects of your legal studies, how you will be evaluated on your performance varies depending upon which law school you attend. In the not-so-distant past, many first-year classes lasted the entire academic year and your grade was based almost entirely on one final exam at the end of the year. Fortunately, legal educators have figured out the learning benefits of having one or more formative assessments before evaluating the sum of students' learning at the end of the course.

Today, your course grade for most first-year classes will be based on, at a minimum, a midterm exam and the final exam. How you perform on the midterm exam will let you know whether you are on the right track, or whether you need to make changes to how you are learning the material and developing your skills.

Law schools in the United States have increasingly moved to even more formative assessments than just the midterm. Many professors will assign practice essays or multiple-choice questions for review or give quizzes and other formative assignments throughout the semester. These assessments and exams are generally weighted, with the greatest weight being given to the final exam at the end of the course. Regardless of the type, frequency, or weight of assessments your professor uses, the key to success is to practice exams in the same way you will be tested.

It's important that you understand the different ways that you can be graded and which of these apply at your law school.

☑️ CRITERION-REFERENCED GRADING

In most undergraduate and graduate programs, students are evaluated based on a criterion-referenced grading system that measures students against a clear set of performance standards that is independent of other students' performance. In a criterion-referenced grading system, you will get what you earn.

A+ GRADING SCALES

There is a wide variety of grading systems in law schools across the United States, with a few of them not awarding any grades at all. Instead these (mostly Ivy League) law schools distinguish student performance by awarding honors, pass/fail, or credit/no credit. Additionally, some schools award letter grades (for example, A+, A, A–) and some use a grade point average (for example, 3.9, 3.0, 2.7).

Grading on the curve

Many law schools use what is called a "relational," or "normalized," grading system. Unlike a criterion-referenced system, your grade is not based solely on your own performance in the course, but on how you performed in relation to other students in the course. In a normalized grading system, students' scores in the course are distributed along a bell curve (hence the expression "grading on the curve") with a certain percentage of scores being awarded a particular grade. For example, students whose scores fall within the top 10% in the course may be awarded an "A," while students whose scores fall within the bottom 10% of the course may receive a failing grade.

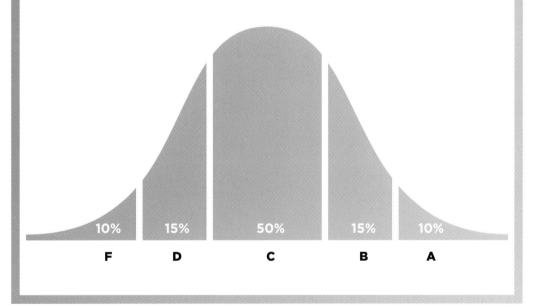

| 10% | 15% | 50% | 15% | 10% |
| F | D | C | B | A |

CLASS RANKINGS

In addition to grades, many law schools rank students graduating in the same year. Your class rank can determine early on your eligibility to obtain or retain financial scholarships, or eligibility for a particular internship. By graduation, your class rank may play a significant role in determining whether you are offered a coveted judicial clerkship or a job at a prestigious law firm.

Regardless of the grading system used in your preferred law school, the competition to be "the best" is ever present and is often the source of great stress and anxiety during exam time. Preparation throughout the term is one of the best ways to avoid stress during exams. Your legal education is yours to claim. Run you own race!

LEARNING TO THINK
LIKE A LAWYER

Much has been said and written about how law school teaches you to "think like a lawyer." This mysterious promise hints at some secret method reserved only for those brave enough to enter into the legal profession. So . . . how does a lawyer think? The most basic, but accurate, answer is: lawyers think critically. They question and challenge, and poke holes in facts and arguments. They evaluate, weigh, and judge law and facts. They dissect and create legal theories and premises. To employ the skill of critical thinking—and it is a skill—is what it means to think like a lawyer.

INDUCTIVE LEARNING

A notable difference between other educational programs and legal education is the way students are trained to learn and think. Have you ever put together a jigsaw puzzle? If you looked at the picture on the box first and used it to build the puzzle, you used deductive learning. This is the way most undergraduate courses are designed. The professor gives you the big picture and then you fit the pieces together for a complete understanding.

In law school, the learning is more inductive. What if you'd never seen the picture on the puzzle box but had built the picture sight unseen? Of course, this method is more challenging. Instead of puzzle pieces, you have legal cases that you must read to build an understanding of the law and the rationale that the courts used. After reading several factually similar cases, you begin to build your understanding of the rule of law. While you don't know how the full picture will look in the end, the process of reading cases will lead you to understand that law intimately by the end of the course.

The art of time management

How do you fit 1,441 tasks in 1,440 minutes? Make a plan! There are 1,440 minutes in a day, and law school can make you feel as if there should be more. Time management is crucial. Using a digital calendar is a great way to plan your day in order to maximize your precious time. Create a daily schedule that includes not only the times of your class meetings, but also times for reading and briefing cases for each class and for updating course outlines or doing practice essay questions. This will increase your likelihood of fitting it all in. See the sample study plan on page 203 to see how much you can achieve with good planning.

THE SOCRATIC METHOD

Reading and understanding the case law is only part of the learning process in law school. It is preparation for another integral part of the learning process: the Socratic method. In essence, the Socratic method of learning involves a structured argumentative discourse among and between students and the professor as a way to stimulate critical thinking. The professor facilitates the discourse by asking you and your fellow students thought-provoking questions about the case law you've read, challenging you to move away from your adopted position and pushing you to perform instant legal analysis to defend it. Through this interactive back and forth, you begin to apply what you've read in the case law and develop a deep understanding of the legal principles. The Socratic method is both exciting and scary for new law students.

Pro tips

PRACTICE MAKES PERFECT

What you will learn in law school is transformational, not informational. This means that learning to think like a lawyer occurs over time. You will not be able to pick up a book, read about it, and then do it. It's a skill that must be practiced. It will involve failure and disappointment at times, but as you progress, you will find that your newfound thinking skills are among the sharpest tools in your legal toolbox.

You may feel uncomfortable being put on the spot in front of the entire class, but consider this training for the practice of law.

A SUCCESSFUL FIRST YEAR

While your law school experience, in many respects, will be uniquely yours, there are a few best practices for learning and achieving in your first year. Remember, countless others before you have run this race and crossed the finish line. If they were able to do it, that means it can be done. If it can be done, then you can do it.

CHECK YOUR EGO AT THE DOOR

There is only one fastest runner in the race, but in a marathon, every finisher is a winner. Setting your goals and standards high is admirable, but setting reasonable expectations will get you through law school. You won't always be right. You won't always get the highest score. Being open to learning is how you win this race.

TRIAL AND ERROR IS THE GAME

One of the best and most consistent ways to learn—be it the law, or parallel parking—is through trial and error. If what you thought would work doesn't, then thoughtfully change what you are doing and try again. Remember, it's a process.

PRACTICE MAKES PERFECT

Taking practice exams is a form of studying throughout the semester. Don't wait until you have to perform to practice what you need to know or do.

BALANCE IS GOLDEN

Work hard; play responsibly. Planning time to relax and enjoy life will help you bounce back after long, arduous hours of studying.

A WINNING MINDSET

Stress is normal in law school but keeping a positive outlook can make your new life a lot easier. Surround yourself with positive affirmations and when times really get tough, remember that you are closer to the finish line than you were yesterday.

"Courage is the most important attribute of a lawyer. It is more important than competence or vision. It can never be an elective in any law school, and it should pervade the heart, the halls of justice, and the chambers of the mind."

Robert F. Kennedy

Pack your common sense and everyday experiences when attending classes and you will be halfway there.

CHAPTER THREE

LEGAL RESEARCH, ANALYSIS, AND WRITING

The late U.S. Supreme Court Justice Ruth Bader Ginsburg once said of lawyers and legal writing, "A lawyer is a skilled professional who has an obligation to serve the public. The more effective a lawyer can be in speech and writing, the better professional he or she will be." Justice Ginsburg implores lawyers to "regard law as an art as well as a craft."

What lawyers do most for their clients and the broader community is communicate. It is critical to be able to do it well. For this reason, most law schools require you to take a series of legal research and writing classes over the course of one year, if not more, to equip yourself with the language and skills to both understand the law and effectively communicate it in writing and through oral advocacy. Moreover, in the United States, the American Bar Association (ABA) requires a legal research, analysis, and writing program in every law school as basic foundational training for law students.

Legal writing differs from the academic writing you did in college, but the skills you learned in preparing papers for college can be adapted to help you succeed in writing for law school and law practice. This chapter explores what legal research and writing entails so you can be prepared for the transition from college to law school prose: the broad goal of legal writing. You will also learn more about the lawyer's role and the importance of understanding the legal system, how to effectively research and understand legal analysis, and about common writing assignments during your first year of law school.

THE BASICS

The broad goal of a legal research, analysis, and writing course in the first year is to integrate legal doctrine, skills, and professional identity for student competency and success. You should expect to do more than simply "write papers." You are likely to explore the following areas.

THE LAWYER'S ROLE

You will learn about the professional responsibility and ethical standards in lawyering, and lawyers' various professional roles in interacting with clients, the judge, the legal system, and the public.

ANALYTICAL WORK

You may explore several approaches to analyzing facts and legal issues. The analytical teaching approach relies on locating the relevant legal authority to predict the resolution of a problem. The problem-based method uses a real or fictional problem to help find a resolution.

THE LEGAL SYSTEM

You will gain a foundational knowledge of the legal system for the country in which you are attending law school. This will include the government structure, primary sources of law, how the sources and law relate to each other, and how the law is applied and enforced.

RESEARCH SKILLS

Your legal research will likely be integrated with your legal writing and analysis problems. You will learn how to conduct effective legal research, both in print and electronically, through commonly available sources and media.

GOOD COMMUNICATION

You will learn how to communicate effectively to a legal audience—for example, a supervising attorney or judge—and to lay persons, such as your client, both in writing and through oral expression.

INTERVIEWING SKILLS

If your law school uses a lawyering skills approach in its legal research and writing curriculum, you will receive instruction on how to interview, counsel, negotiate, engage in alternative dispute resolution, and draft common legal documents.

"The practice of law requires accurate and precise analysis of facts, legal issues, and authorities, as well as effective communication of that analysis."

ABA, Legal Writing Sourcebook

KEY SKILLS

While effective legal writing is very important for your legal practice, there are additional skills new lawyers are expected to have during their first year of practice. These skills are integrated within your first year legal research, analysis, and writing curriculum. The top 10 skills considered necessary in the short term, in order of importance are as follows:

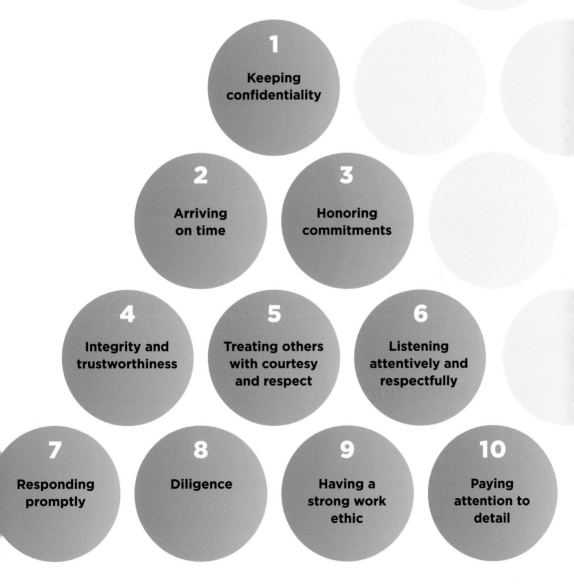

1 Keeping confidentiality

2 Arriving on time

3 Honoring commitments

4 Integrity and trustworthiness

5 Treating others with courtesy and respect

6 Listening attentively and respectfully

7 Responding promptly

8 Diligence

9 Having a strong work ethic

10 Paying attention to detail

LEGAL WRITING FLOW

The number of assignments you will have in your legal writing course will depend on how many credits the course is given, how many semesters of legal writing are required, and the professor-to-student ratio.

Typically, a common flow of legal research and writing instruction in the first year moves through one or more predictive memoranda and related exercises, toward a persuasive brief or motion, and an oral advocacy exercise. If the legal writing course integrates more advanced skills to prepare you for law practice, you may also: draft a research log; plan or outline, e-mail memos, client letters, or contracts; and engage in a negotiation or related exercise.

FIRST SEMESTER

Short writing and analysis assignments and predictive (or objective) memoranda tend to be the focus of the first semester, along with developing the necessary skills for achieving successful results.

SHORT WRITING AND ANALYSIS ASSIGNMENTS

These introduce you to the critical skills of analyzing individual cases to understand how a court interprets existing law to resolve an issue based on specific facts. You'll learn to synthesize several cases to learn key ideas or broader themes and to identify several types of legal reasoning (for example, rule-based or policy). Usually given as "closed memo" assignments, these may be written in a traditional legal memorandum format (see pages 44–45) or, as is becoming more common in practice, an e-mail memorandum.

PREDICTIVE MEMORANDA

The predictive (or objective) memo is often the capstone assignment at the end of the first semester of the first year. This assignment builds on the critical skills learned at the start of the semester—analyzing a select number of cases and grappling with legal reasoning. By and large, these are usually "open memo" assignments. This assignment is called predictive, or objective, because you are trying to predict, based on your research, how a court might resolve the legal issue for your client.

RESEARCH EXERCISES

Every legal issue a court resolves requires governing rules, thus the goal of research for every assignment is finding the relevant law. Today, it is common for research to be conducted online, but many law schools and legal organizations have hard copies of commonly used legal sources for their specific practice area, so it is important that you understand how to effectively research both online and in print. Effective research takes time and practice—there is no shortcut to this process, not even for seasoned lawyers—and it is a necessary and critical skill to understand in the first year of law school.

CITATION EXERCISES

Another critical component of legal writing is the requirement to support a given interpretation of the law with legal authority. When you wrote academic papers in college and relied on sources other than yourself, you supported those statements with the source information, or "proof" of who said it. Legal writing requires similar proof of authority. In the first year, you will likely rely on cases, statutes, and constitutions as "proof" for the legal rules and legal reasoning they draft in assignments. In more advanced writing courses, you may also rely on other sources, such as articles, encyclopedias, reports, and so forth.

Assignment terminology

Closed memo
Students are given the sources to prepare short writing and analysis assignments, so they can focus on analyzing a single element of a larger rule, based on a few cases.

Open memo
Students are tasked with doing their own research to find relevant case law and legal rules.

E-mail memorandum
A more streamlined version of a traditional legal memorandum focused on both casual (but still professional) tone and brevity for the fast-paced world of electronic communication.

SECOND SEMESTER

Persuasion and advocacy tend to be the focus of the legal reseach, analysis, and writing course during the second semester of the first year at law school.

CLIENT INTERVIEWS

Client interviewing, or counseling, is a skill that may be incorporated into the first semester but is very common in the second semester of legal writing. Usually attached to a larger legal writing assignment, the exercise allows you to interview your professor, teacher assistant, or a hired actor, to learn the facts for a particular assignment. Client interviews are intended to simulate real practice.

PERSUASIVE WRITING ASSIGNMENT

Having obtained the facts from either a written document or a client-interview simulation, you then use those facts to research the legal issue facing your client. Distinct from the predictive memo in the first semester, the persuasive writing assignment requires you to serve as the lawyer for a specific side and argue for a resolution that favors your client. The assignment usually takes the form of a motion, or trial, or appellate brief.

ORAL ARGUMENT

Having drafted your persuasive motion or brief, you may then be called upon to argue the merits of your motion or brief before a "judge," again simulating real practice. The oral argument may be a single exercise within each legal writing class, or it may be conducted school-wide across the entire first-year class and involve preliminary, semi-, and final rounds. The broader goal of the oral argument is to allow you to engage in oral advocacy.

NEGOTIATION AND DRAFTING EXERCISE

A negotiation and drafting exercise may serve as a final capstone to the persuasive writing assignment and oral argument, or it may be set as an independent exercise. Here, you represent a client on opposite sides of a legal issue, negotiating on behalf of your client. You then draft a written agreement that reflects the terms and conditions the parties adopted as the complete and final expression of their negotiated or mediated agreement.

> **Simulation exercises will help you to develop key skills in client communication and representation.**

LEGAL MEMORANDA

Legal memoranda are used to inform the intended audience about the law, predict the outcome, and determine next steps. While you will write these memoranda for your professor during law school, in legal practice you will write them for your supervising attorney, other lawyers you work with, or, in some cases, the client.

THE TRADITIONAL FORMAT

This document can preserve your thoughts on the case and provide a starting point for updating the document with new facts or additional research. In practice the format may be modified to fit the needs of the supervising attorney or office, but the traditional format shown opposite is a common starting point used in legal writing courses. The organization is akin to a classical speech: introduce the issue, state your position on the issue, state the nature of the dispute, build your case, refute adversarial claims, and conclude.

DRAFTING THE LEGAL ANALYSIS

There are common frameworks that many law professors rely upon in helping students find a logical organization for drafting the analysis in the "discussion" section of a legal memorandum. The most common is called "IRAC," which stands for: Issue, Rule, Application, and Conclusion. Other frameworks derive from IRAC, all with the aim of reminding students of additional aspects to include in the final analysis. Some iterations, for example, use an "E" for Explanation (IREAC), "C" for Conclusion (CRAC/CREAC), or "T" for Thesis (TREAT). It is important to understand that there is no "magic" formula for drafting the legal analysis, however. Some professors use the IRAC frameworks to help organize,

but the outline cannot fill in the depth necessary for a strong analysis. Rather, there are important questions to consider at each step of the legal analysis process, and these will influence what is included or excluded, and the final arrangement of information based upon both client and situation.

Key questions to consider

★ How many legal issues will be analyzed?

★ What are the relevant rules for each legal issue?

★ Are there helpful cases from the past that illustrate how a rule functions?

★ How does a rule apply to the client's facts in light of how the rule has functioned in the past?

★ What will the other side argue?

★ How is the court likely to resolve the argument?

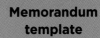
Memorandum template

HEADING

Includes who wrote the memo, to whom, for what purpose, and date written.

QUESTION PRESENTED

Sets forth the legal issue being analyzed.

BRIEF ANSWER

Summarizes your answer to the legal issue, and may include a brief excerpt of the relevant law and brief conclusion.

STATEMENT OF FACTS

Sets forth the client's legally relevant background and procedural facts.

DISCUSSION

Offers a detailed analysis of each legal issue. Professors vary on the analytical framework they prefer students to use in arranging this section. Regardless of the organization, the content typically includes the following:

- Issue or conclusion statement
- Rule paragraph
- Explanation of any relevant case law
- Application of the law to your client's facts
- Discussion of your opponent's position with rebuttal
- Policy implications (if relevant)
- Conclusion, including next steps

CONCLUSION

Summarizes your analysis on the legal issue.

LEGAL WRITING IN PRACTICE

Strong legal research, analysis, and writing skills are the foundation of any career you might pursue as a lawyer. Every area of law (criminal, family, or business, for example) will require the need to research specific issues and communicate that information either in writing or through oral expression to a client, colleague, judge, or the broader public. There are two primary keys to success.

YOUR CLASSROOM KNOWLEDGE

Owing to the demands of practice, such as having a large volume of cases, needing to respond quickly to clients, and adhering to deadlines imposed by courts, you will often be required to produce quality work in a short time frame. This work must be accurate and precise.

In many ways, a legal writing course in law school is a simulation course that prepares you for legal practice. You will begin with easier assignments, focusing perhaps on just one or two skills, and then gradually receive more challenging assignments that both build on the previous skills and, in many cases, require you to transfer those skills to new problems. Your ability to bring your classroom knowledge into practice is vital to your success as a lawyer.

FINDING YOUR OWN VOICE

Within the formal, and sometimes technical, aspects of learning legal writing, there can be a tension between learning it "right" and using your own words to communicate. In other words, while legal writing is a genre that has a familiar language and patterns that are unique to its members, it is possible to respect and understand the genre and its conventions, and still use your authentic voice in expressing an analysis.

The letter opposite is from a student who came to the realization that legal writing was far more than a technical endeavor, but also required a conscious awareness of the depth of legal analysis and the value of using one's authentic voice. This conscious awareness of legal analysis as an interactive process moves students quickly beyond any formulaic writing and helps them ask questions at each stage of the analysis in order to produce more intentional and thoughtful legal writing. Consider this analytical process as a "rhetorical profile" that combines the art of communication/persuasion (rhetoric) with a summary of processing questions for effective legal analysis and stronger legal writing.

Dear Professor Culver,

I hope this email finds you and your family well and managing under the current events. I am writing to share, what I hope, is some good news.

I recently had my "Eureka!" moment for what it means to "think like a lawyer," while working on a memo for California Motion Drafting and Procedure, and I am writing to thank you for your role in that revelation.

In year one, I followed all of the axioms for what people say it means to be a good lawyer — writing in the active voice; researching the legal issues; and applying facts to understand the law of an issue. So, I was confused when I got the feedback that I was a "good writer," but my grades never reflected how "good" I was. What I failed to understand then was that people really meant that I was a good "technical" writer — that is, grammarian. And while writing in the "active voice" is a prerequisite to being a good legal writer, I see that doing so does not necessarily make one a competent, let alone good, legal writer.

Here's where your introduction of the concept of the "rhetorical profile" comes in. I can now fully appreciate its brilliance for legal writing and the relationship between legal research, objective writing in memos, and effective advocacy.

Joe McFinley, Third-year student

PART

NAVIGATING
LAW SCHOOL

CHAPTER FOUR

YOUR SECOND YEAR

Now that you have completed the first lap of law school, it's time to prepare for the second leg of your journey! You gained momentum in the first year, but now it's time to build your stamina so you can finish strong in your final year. To make sure you meet your goal, every step in your journey requires a good map to guide your way and a good cadence to keep your pace.

No runner who wants to win the race sits down to take a break one-third of the way through the course! Neither does a winner decide that they can lay back and coast the rest of the way. Every year of law school is a progressive stage in your development so there is never a time to sit down or coast if you plan to reach the finish line strong. Making it through the first year is challenging but hold on tight! It's time to catch your second wind and step up the pace. It's only the second year. The race is not over yet!

"The first year, they scare you to death. The second year, they work you to death. The third year, they bore you to death." This is a common myth passed down through the generations to law students today. The truth is . . . law school is what you make it. This chapter discusses how degree planning, course selection, concentration areas, practicums, and dual degrees can help you build an exciting and relevant educational plan. The second year of law school is your opportunity to begin to link your knowledge and skills to the practice of law. Take advantage of these opportunities to get a head start on your career!

YOUR DEGREE PLAN

For anything that is worth spending time and money on, developing a strong plan for success is key. Your law degree is no different. Some students know early on the area in which they plan to work once they qualify to practice law. Other students simply know that they want to practice law. Even practicing attorneys sometimes shift their areas of practice years into their careers.

BEFORE LAW SCHOOL

It is perfectly fine to develop a specific interest in the law after your legal education begins, but there is still room to plan the basics before you arrive or during your first year. A good place to start is with Chapter Eight: After the Race, which offers an overview of the options available to you. Use the template on page 201 to start building a picture of your degree plan.

RESEARCHING YOUR PATH

The practice of law can be taxing work even for one who loves the law. Therefore, your chosen practice area should include interests or passions that are independent of the practice of law. For example:

★ If you have a passion for protecting the rights of elderly people, you may decide to practice elder law.
★ If you are a person who is passionate about crime and punishment, you may want to consider a career as a prosecutor or criminal defense attorney.

The applications for your legal degree are extremely vast and wide, as nearly every aspect of our daily lives are governed, or impacted, by laws.

> **"A good plan is like a roadmap; it shows the final destination and usually the best way to get there."**
>
> H. Stanley Judd, American author

IDENTIFYING YOUR FIELD OF INTEREST

A simple search of careers for attorneys in your region or country is a good place to begin. For example, a quick search for legal practice areas in the United States returns a list of sites dedicated to helping you research different legal areas and what is required to practice in those areas. One of these, the Law School Admissions Council's Discover Law page, lists 16 legal fields that you can explore. There's even a quiz to help you get started in discovering your path.

AT LAW SCHOOL

Most law schools have academic advisors to assist students in planning their degrees. Your advisors may be faculty or administrators who specialize in advising. Be proactive in seeking guidance from your advisor. Ideally, you should make an appointment once or twice each term to discuss your progress and ideas about extracurricular or cocurricular activities that can boost your academic experience.

GRADUATION REQUIREMENTS

Many countries, local jurisdictions, and law schools have additional graduation requirements, such as a significant scholarly writing assignment and experiential learning activities in the form of internships or externships. Your academic advisor should partner with you to make sure that all of your graduation requirements are being met throughout law school and that you are on track for a timely graduation. See also, Chapter Five: Legal Writing and Research Beyond the First Year and Chapter Twelve: Internships and Externships.

THE STUDENT PERSPECTIVE

Upper-level students at your school may be good sources of information when it comes to planning your degree. They have already traveled the road you are on and can provide valuable information about courses, professors, and experiential opportunities. You may find that some of the more adventurous students have enrolled in study programs abroad or visited other law schools in order to broaden their exposure to areas of practice or career opportunities.

Pro tips

NETWORKING

Getting to know people from a wide variety of backgrounds in the legal sphere will help expand your knowledge of the legal profession and to gain insight via other people's experiences. As the 21st century progresses, virtual networking will only push your boundaries further: "If I had to pick one thing you gain [from virtual conferencing] it's the instant ability to connect and learn from people around the world in real time. Face-to-face you listen to speakers and meet interesting people in the coffee line but online you can actually interact in really deep ways with one another."
Dave McLeod, CEO of Thoughtexchange.
For more on networking, see Chapter Ten.

YOUR PRIORITIES

TYPE OF PRACTICE

Solo practice brings the freedom to balance professional and personal life. A large firm is a good place to land for a higher starting salary and partnership in the longer term. Public interest law can fulfill an altruistic urge to serve the public. In-house counsel positions are generally less hectic than those in a large firm but provide the steady income that may take a while to build with a solo practice.

SALARY

Salary is important but don't forget there's more to life than money. Your family life and financial needs can be a driving factor in choosing your first job. Some new lawyers choose a lower-paying public interest job during the first 10 years of practice in order to take advantage of student loan forgiveness programs. Others opt for a fast-paced, high-paying job at a large firm before they begin to build a family.

EMERGING FIELDS

As new technology and new issues develop, so does the need for lawyers to develop and shape the law in those areas. Emerging fields of practice provide an opportunity to get ahead of the legal curve in areas such as pandemic law, artificial intelligence law, and data protection and privacy law.

WORK/LIFE BALANCE

We all enter the practice of law at various stages in our lives. What work/life balance looks like for a new 23-year-old attorney with no spouse or children may be very different than how it looks for a 35-year-old new attorney with a spouse and four young children or a 50-year-old, second-career attorney with elderly parents. Reflect on your needs and what is really important for your work/life balance.

NEGLECTED JURISDICTIONS

Much has been said and written in the last 10 years about the overabundance of lawyers in society; however, there are actually plenty of places that have a shortage of lawyers. If you yearn for the small town life, you may find it much easier to set up a practice than you think.

BEYOND YOUR LAW SCHOOL

Don't be afraid to look beyond your law school for courses and/or experiential opportunities that will help develop your areas of interest further.

ASK A PROFESSIONAL

Once you have narrowed down a few areas of interest, reach out to attorneys who are practicing in those fields. Many attorneys relish the opportunity to share their knowledge, experiences, and viewpoints with students and to serve as advisors and mentors. See also pages 126–127: Informational Interviews.

"Don't be afraid to take advice. There's always something new to learn."

Babe Ruth, legendary American baseball player

TRAVELING FARTHER AFIELD

As you develop your areas of interest in the law, you may find that your law school has only a limited number or type of related courses, but another law school may have a much broader and deeper selection of courses available. Most law schools provide opportunities for their students to "visit" other law schools for one or more academic terms. The number of courses or units you can take at another law school is determined by your home school.

Choosing where to visit depends on your legal interests. Often, the needs of a particular state, province, or region will drive the choice of available courses or experiential opportunities. For example, in the United States, oil and gas law is a practice area that is much more relevant in the state of Texas than it is in the state of Ohio, so the availability of courses in those topics is more prevalent in Texas law schools.

In addition to this, individual law schools may have partnerships or programming schedules with foreign law schools that provide opportunities for students to visit during the summer or other academic terms. Students who have visited or participated in these outside programs can provide a unique perspective as you plan your degree.

COURSE **SELECTION**

While the courses you take in the first year of law school are generally set in stone, you will have several interesting courses (electives) to choose from in your second and third years of study. The types of courses that your school offers may be unique to the region, industry, or simply the professional interests of your professors.

THE ROLE OF ELECTIVES

While your first-year foundational courses focus on the most common legal principles and practice areas, elective courses add substance to your degree and prepare you to practice in a variety of legal areas. Which electives are right for your degree plan will depend on your legal areas of interest and the needs of the community in which you plan to practice.

Pro tips

USEFUL RESOURCES

★ Your law school should maintain a list of all elective courses that are regularly taught, as well as special-topic electives that may be offered periodically.

★ Many schools provide a schedule of offered courses one or two years in advance so that students can plan their degrees early.

★ Look for information on electives in your school's catalog, the registrar's office, or posted on the school's website.

LEGAL CONCENTRATIONS

When it comes to electives, many law schools offer clusters of courses that allow students to focus their course work and practical experience toward a specialized legal practice. Legal concentrations are great if you are passionate about a particular legal area or know exactly what type of law you want to practice. They can also make your resume stand out to employers with practices in the same area.

If your law school does not have established concentrations, you may be able to build a concentration by choosing elective courses and internships that are related to, and support, your area of interest. Participating in live-client clinics and visiting or taking electives at other law schools can help fill the gaps in a legal concentration that exists at your own school. Be creative and always work closely with your academic advisor.

Concentration:
Real estate law and transactions

Courses:
Real property law
Land use and zoning law
Water rights law
Real estate transactions
Real estate securities and
foreclosure law

Concentration:
Intellectual property

Courses:
Intellectual property overview
Copyright law
Trademark law
Patent law
International intellectual
property law

Concentration:
Estate planning

Courses:
Decedent estates
Wills and trusts
State or federal tax law
Will and trust drafting
Guardian and conservatorships
Probate practicum

Bar exam courses

At the end of your legal education, you will likely be required to pass a bar (licensing) examination. While many companies offer post-graduation exam review and preparation courses tailored to specific jurisdictions, most of the subjects tested on bar exams are also offered in law school either as required or elective courses.

Selecting courses in law school that are tested on the bar exam is beneficial because they provide early and repeated exposure to the subject for a deeper level of understanding.

Commercial exam preparation courses offer a quick and comprehensive review of exam subjects, so taking those same courses in law school can provide a strong foundation to support the review during exam preparation.

Consider the difficulty of the exam-tested subject and how frequently it appears on the bar exam. Also note that each jurisdiction may have different subjects tested on their bar exam. For example, in California, professional responsibility is always tested because it is required under the California Bar rules. In Texas, oil and gas law is often tested due to the prevalence of the petroleum industry. It certainly is not necessary to take every subject that is tested on the bar exam while you are in law school but it is wise to know your options. See also Chapter Seven: Taking the Bar Exam.

PRACTICUMS

A practicum provides a supervised practice application for the theoretical portion of a course so that you can get hands-on experience in a practice area in which you are interested.

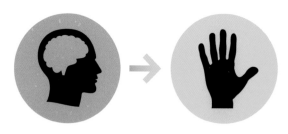

For example, a course in family law will address the legal principles established by statutes and case law, while an accompanying practicum in family law may teach you how to complete forms used in family court, negotiate custody agreements between parents, or draft property settlement agreements. Many courses in law school are suitable as a practicum course; however, class sizes tend to be small (8 to 12) so that students get individualized attention. Courses can focus on a particular practice area or on a particular skill set, such as legal writing, being in-house counsel, civil litigation, or managing a solo practice.

Practicum courses can use real or hypothetical cases and clients and are often considered by prospective employers as work experience.

DUAL AND JOINT DEGREES

Many law schools offer dual- and/or joint-degree programs. While the terms are often used interchangeably, they are technically different. A dual degree involves getting two different degrees from two different universities or colleges at the same time (for example, JD/MBA), while a joint degree is generally one degree that is designed collaboratively between two universities or colleges.

Having two degrees is great, but if you are not going to use both to enhance your career, a dual-degree program may not be ideal. Consider whether it is worth the extra cost in time and possibly money.

Pro tips

PLAN AHEAD

If you are interested in a dual or joint degree, speak to both your law school advisor and your advisor for the dual degree program about the eligibility requirements either before law school or during your first year. This will give you time to consider which degree to pair with your JD and how to work the classes for your second degree into your JD program. You will need to make sure the classes you take in the joint or dual degree program will actually count as electives for the JD degree.

"The practical experience students gain in practicum courses is invaluable to a balanced program of legal education."

CHAPTER FIVE

LEGAL RESEARCH AND WRITING BEYOND THE FIRST YEAR

The American Bar Association (ABA) requires that each student "satisfactorily complete" at least "one additional writing experience after the first year." As such, most law schools offer numerous elective courses during the second and third years that provide additional opportunities for students to expand on their writing experience.

This chapter looks at common ways in which second- and third-year law students engage in upper-level legal writing and research beyond the first year: advanced legal writing and research courses; legal drafting; judicial-opinion writing; and scholarly writing through seminars and law review. Collectively, these upper-level courses offer students experiences that the required first-year course cannot. Some legal writing and research course offerings may be required in order to graduate, and others will be optional.

What these writing opportunities have in common is to provide more breadth into concepts introduced in the first year of law school. While these advanced courses fall broadly under the umbrella of upper-level legal research and writing, the courses can vary in terms of their scope to offer a writing experience versus writing instruction. Gaining additional writing experience after the first year of law school is essential, and as upper-level students, you should take advantage of any opportunity to take your legal writing to the next level!

ADVANCED LEGAL WRITING AND RESEARCH

Even the best legal research, analysis, and writing courses in the first year are constrained, due to time and resources. They do not offer students sufficient opportunities to master the concepts they have learned during this time and are even less likely to introduce them to other legal writing formats. Thus, some schools require a third semester of advanced writing as part of the mandatory legal writing instruction in the first year (see Chapter Two).

This third semester usually takes place during the second year of law school. This advanced instruction provides greater depth into concepts introduced in the first and second semesters. Expect to delve deeper into the following areas.

LEGAL RESEARCH

Instruction builds on the foundational legal research instruction given in the first year and explores advanced research tools broadly or related to a particular area of law. Such specialized areas may include legislative history, administrative regulations, specialty publications, practice manuals, jury instructions, and international sources.

PREDICTIVE (OBJECTIVE) WRITING

Instruction builds on the predictive writing practiced in the first year. You'll also explore advanced aspects of effective memo writing, including sophisticated research and legal analysis.

"Much, indeed most, of the communication that lawyers engage in is written. To write well is to communicate well. To write poorly is to communicate poorly. It also matters because to the extent that lawyers don't write well, to the extent they abuse words, to the extent they use them incorrectly, they are making dull the tools of their trade, which is a terrible thing."

The late United States Supreme Court Justice Antonin Scalia

WAYS TO BUILD ON YOUR SKILLS

★ Read good writing. "The best teachers of writing are good writers who you read . . . " United States Supreme Court Justice John G. Roberts.

★ Watch or listen to the oral arguments of former United States Supreme Court Justices when they were practicing; or oral arguments of other lawyers with a reputation for strong oral advocacy skills.

★ Read judicial opinions by judges or justices well known for strong, artful, and persuasive legal writing skills. As a form of persuasive writing, judicial opinions serve as an illustration of specific persuasive writing strategies.

PERSUASIVE WRITING

Instruction builds on persuasive writing techniques learned in the first year and explores theoretical principles of human nature that support techniques and strategies of persuasion. Three fundamental processes of persuasion, stemming from classical rhetoric, are logos, pathos, and ethos. Logos is persuasion through logic and rational argument, using established legal authorities. Persuading through logos is the most common method of persuasive writing that students learn during their traditional introductory legal writing courses. Pathos is persuasion through emotion. And ethos is persuasion by establishing credibility before the audience.

APPELLATE ADVOCACY

Instruction builds on the motion/brief and oral argument instruction received in the first year. You'll explore more sophisticated aspects of brief writing, rules of appellate procedure, and advanced skills in appellate argument (see the following pages for more on this).

"As a lawyer, you hope to be prepared for questions, to understand where they lead, to have thought several moves ahead, so that you can answer correctly, rather than just sort of on the spur of the moment."

United States Supreme Court Justice John G. Roberts on the preparation necessary for oral arguments

ADVANCED APPELLATE ADVOCACY

Advanced appellate advocacy is a common advanced legal research and writing course. The term "appellate" relates to an appeal, as when a client wants a decision of a lower (or trial) court to be reviewed by a higher court. That higher court is called an appellate court. Appellate advocacy is when a lawyer represents a client before a court that hears appeals. See also pages 102–103: The Appellate Attorney.

INSIDE THE APPELLATE COURT

One key difference between a trial court and an appellate court is that in the appellate court there are no longer juries, witnesses, presentation of evidence, and so forth. Rather, those attending appellate court only have "the record" before them—that is, the written transcript of what happened at trial. So, when an appellate attorney seeks to persuade the appellate court toward a particular outcome, they must do so through effective and persuasive written briefs and oral arguments.

YOUR ROLE

How do the workings of the appellate court affect you? Crafting your legal research and writing skills becomes extremely important; your client's freedom may depend on it. An advanced appellate advocacy course helps students understand the important and intentional decisions that must be made in drafting briefs for the court, and for the law clerks who will more than likely be the primary brief readers.

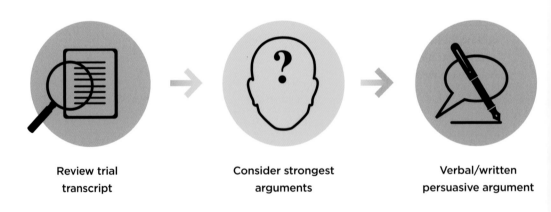

| Review trial transcript | Consider strongest arguments | Verbal/written persuasive argument |

"If you look at the really good advocates, they know what their two or three major points are, their central arguments are, and maybe something that they need to tease out a little bit from the briefs, and they stick to it. And they could take you right back to it with all the cacophony."

United States Supreme Court Justice Clarence Thomas

PERSUASIVE WRITTEN ADVOCACY

1 Start strong
Let your introduction clearly indicate why you should win. Don't waste time telling the court why you are there.

2 Make it personal
Consider using full party names for all concerned, instead of party labels such as "plaintiff" and "defendant."

3 Exercise decorum
Stay classy. Never attempt to belittle the other side, but stay civil whatever the circumstances.

4 Keep it brief
Avoid excessive wordiness. Use short sentences and phrases; don't waste space with too many or long words.

5 Employ graphics
Consider including visual content where appropriate. This can help counter dry legal analysis.

6 Avoid legalese
This is the "lawyerly" language that sounds stuffy (for example, "heretofore"; see also page 67).

7 Don't fawn
Do not be nauseating in your language. For example, don't use "Defendant respectfully submits," as opposed to "Defendant contends."

8 Write well
Brush up on your basic grammar. For example, know when to use "that" or "which" and "who" and "whom."

9 Cite well
Be succinct when citing cases. Make the reason for your reliance on the case clear and simple.

10 Cite appropriately
Put citations in the text, not in footnotes as you would in a scholarly article. Judges do not want to hunt for the authority to support your proposition.

SEMINARS, DRAFTING, AND JUDICIAL OPINION WRITING

Students enter the realm of scholarly legal writing through writing for law review and writing papers in upper-division seminars taken in the second and third years. Judges, practicing attorneys, legislators, and advocacy groups draw upon scholarly legal writing to help them write informed opinions and better advocate for clients and constituents.

In addition to scholarly legal writing, you can also take courses on other types of legal documents that lawyers prepare during practice or judicial clerkships, such as legal drafting and judicial opinion writing. What these writing opportunities have in common is to provide more breadth into concepts introduced in the first year of law school.

Unlike the depth of advanced legal writing instruction courses, however, many scholarly seminars, drafting, and judicial opinion courses at best provide only a writing experience, as opposed to instruction, due to the demand to balance teaching a substantive area of law alongside the legal writing to showcase it.

SEMINARS

The most common upper-level writing experience is where students write a scholarly paper on a topic related to a seminar subject, or as an independent study with faculty supervision.

Student scholarly writing is intended to mimic the rigorous writing and research done regularly by law professors, practitioners, and judges who critically think about the law and write law review articles to help shape the law. See pages 68–69 for a more in-depth discussion on Scholarly Writing.

LEGAL DRAFTING

Distinct from courses on legal writing, where communication is often between members of a law firm (predictive) or advocacy to the court (persuasive), courses on legal drafting demonstrate how practicing lawyers can communicate with their clients or other parties. In legal drafting courses, therefore, writing instruction emphasizes the fundamental conventions for drafting documents, including:

★ audience

★ tone

★ key terms

★ plain language

★ practice-area-specific features

Some example courses also focus on the following areas, among others:

- ★ contract drafting
- ★ business drafting
- ★ patent document drafting
- ★ real estate drafting
- ★ estate planning drafting

JUDICIAL OPINION WRITING

The opportunity to engage in judicial opinion writing is a relatively new concept as an advanced legal writing course for many law schools, thus academic instruction is not widespread.

But in this upper-level writing experience, students would examine judicial opinions for the following elements:

- ★ unique format and structure
- ★ argument and policy inclusion
- ★ the opinion's reach and impact

Legalese

One of the primary critiques of legal writing has been the onslaught of superfluous language and legal jargon (legalese) that makes the law difficult for the average person to understand. In fact, United States Supreme Court Justice John G. Robert, when asked about legal writing in the 19th century, stated:

"Well, you have good writers in every era. And certainly our profession has gone through periods . . . It's the same with contracts. You can look at an old contract, and it's filled with jargon and legalese and whereas and heretofore, and you just wonder why they didn't just . . . People didn't talk that way, and why they felt compelled to shift into a different language when they were writing a contract . . . ."

One thing that students might encounter in a legal drafting course, therefore, is finding ways to simplify the language so that contracts are easier to understand.

This course can be very helpful for students seeking to become judicial law clerks. See also, Chapter Thirteen: Judicial Clerkships.

SCHOLARLY WRITING

Scholarly writing differs from the writing students do during the first year legal writing, research, and analytical course in two significant ways.

First, scholarly writing is not instrumental writing. The foundational legal writing practiced during the first year focuses on drafting legal documents that relate to a client's legal issue. Second, unlike the narrow purpose of instrumental writing—that is, presenting or defending the client's legal issue, scholarly writing is intended to share your ideas with the broader legal community, and hopefully impact how they think about the law and who is harmed or benefitted by the law. It should also contribute to legal conversations in a meaningful way.

SEMINARS

Given the tremendous learning benefits of scholarly writing, it makes sense that it is woven into a significant amount of the second- and third-year curriculum through seminars. One reason for the myriad of seminars is due to law professors' ability to choose whether to require a final exam or a paper at the end of the course. Further, because many law professors teach multiple courses in the law school, they may balance an exam course with a writing requirement course. Another reason includes the reality that writing

"Find one new point, one new insight, one new way of looking at a piece of law, and organize your entire article around that."

Professor Richard Delgado

THE SCHOLARLY WRITING PROCESS

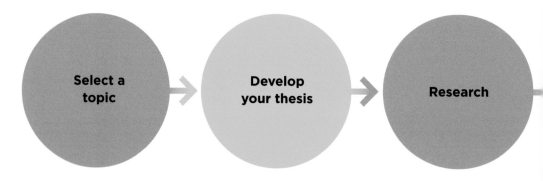

Select a topic → Develop your thesis → Research

requirement courses are permitted to be smaller in size (sometimes less than 15 students) to permit more intensive revision and feedback on students' papers.

Though scholarly writing seminars are the most common avenue to satisfy the upper-level legal writing requirement in U.S. law schools, there is emerging wisdom that, because only a small percentage of law students become law professors—the primary drafters of law review articles—focusing extensively on scholarly writing in law school is misguided. For this reason, think strongly about varying your second- and third-year courses not only with scholarly seminars of interest, but also with advanced legal writing courses that increase the depth of your writing skills.

LAW REVIEW

A more competitive avenue to obtain scholarly writing experience is through the law school's law review. Essentially, this is a periodical that contains articles written by professors, practicing attorneys, and even judges. The purpose, as is common to scholarly writing generally, is to offer opinions on the law, or where the law is absent, that help to shape the future of the profession and broader society.

To be on law review is a prestigious honor. The process usually involves a grade-on or write-on competition at the end of your first year, and the membership is comprised of a small number of second- and third-year students, and a faculty advisor.

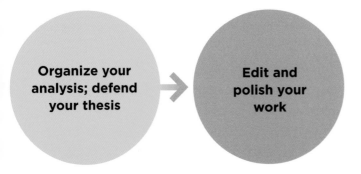

Organize your analysis; defend your thesis → Edit and polish your work

CHAPTER SIX

YOUR THIRD YEAR

Two down and one to go! With two-thirds of law school behind you, you are probably thinking, "This wasn't so hard after all!" Memories of the terror of the unknowns in the first year and the quickened pace of the second are beginning to fade away as the finish line appears in the distance. As you gaze toward the end of your journey, savor the moment and reflect on everything that has gone into preparing you for this time.

Just when you thought it was safe to slow down, you round the bend to the final year of law school. The third year of law school is filled with the excitement and anticipation of nearing the end of your journey. Graduation and family celebrations loom near. The final year is where all of your law school experiences begin to settle and gel into something resembling a finish line. There remain a host of lessons to learn and tasks to complete but your focus will begin to turn more fully to your professional life beyond law school—a journey that began in the first year. Each step of the way, you have added to the richness of your career in the law. But first, the final test!

Contrary to the myth, the final year of law school is anything BUT boring! This chapter provides tips for making your final year productive, including maximizing the support your law school offers as you prepare for the bar (licensing) exam and your entry into the legal profession. There is still important work to be done before graduating and taking the bar exam, such as timely completion of the necessary applications for your state's bar exam, financing the exam, securing time off to study, and enlisting support from your family and friends. Don't stop running before you reach the finish line!

TOWARD THE BAR EXAM

The final year of law school signifies a shift from the ways in which courses are taught in previous years, with a deep dive into statutes, case law, policy, and theory to very focused preparation for the licensing exam. Attorney licensing exams in the United States are collectively called the "bar exam." Exams for law school courses are significantly different than bar exams. It's important to understand how your law school's exams may differ so that you can begin the transition from the way you were tested in law school, to the way you will be tested on the bar exam.

The final year in law school is the year in which students begin to plan their study for the bar exam and for the job that comes after. Many law schools have courses or programs to support this transition. Taking full advantage of the resources your school offers can make this transition easier.

Making an early leap from the way you study and write exams in law school to the way you will study and write exams for professional licensure can help ensure your success on the biggest exam of your life. See also Chapter Seven: Taking the Bar Exam.

Pro tips

DO THE GROUNDWORK

Your law school journey began with research and planning and that is how your quest for your license should begin. Visit the state bar website for the jurisdiction where you plan to take the bar exam and check out:

★ The eligibility requirements for licensing, including educational requirements

★ The legal subjects tested on the exam; are there any that are required to be tested in every exam administration?

★ The dates the exam is administered

★ The location(s) of the exam; some states have one exam location and others have multiple locations

★ Commercial bar review providers

Know the difference

The following are some examples of how a bar exam may differ from law school exams:

★ While law school professors are adept at crafting exam questions for their courses, most are not specifically trained in writing the style of questions you will see on the bar exam.

★ Some law school exams may not include a particular exam format that is used on a bar exam (for example, the performance test on American bar exams).

★ Law school exams generally test only the law covered in the course. For example, in a course on the law of torts, you can rest assured that only the subject of torts will be tested on the final exam. To the contrary, bar exams cover multiple subjects in one exam, some of which you may never have taken during law school. In fact, the bar exam will not even identify the legal subject that is being addressed in each question.

★ Law school exams usually last a few hours, whereas a bar exam can last a few days.

★ Law school exams may be open book or open note. Bar exams are not. Examinees are not allowed to use notes or other study aids.

★ Law school exams are generally low-stake exams. Conceivably, a student can fail the final exam and still pass the course if he/she scores very well on the other course assessments. Bar exams are high stakes in terms of job loss if you fail, financial loss in terms of paying to retake the exam, and the emotional cost of humiliation and depression.

"Before anything else, preparation is the key to success."

Alexander Graham Bell, American inventor

EARLY BAR EXAM PREPARATION COURSES

Early bar exam preparation courses have become more popular over the years, especially in the United States. This is largely due to the American Bar Association's (ABA) requirement that law schools maintain a minimum bar pass rate for the two-year period after a class of students graduates. Failing to meet this minimum bar passage standard could result in a school being placed on probation and possibly losing its national or local accreditation. Consequently, more schools have developed early bar preparation courses to help students pass the bar exam on their first attempt.

WHEN TO TAKE THE COURSE

If given the choice of taking an early exam preparation course in law school, there are advantages to taking it in either the penultimate or ultimate term before graduation. Consider whether you will need more time to process the volume of information and exam strategies between

WHEN TO TAKE EARLY BAR PREPARATION?

PENULTIMATE TERM

Pros

- Earlier identification of weaknesses means more time to work on them before the exam
- Less demanding on private life
- You can plan more effectively
- Less stressful mentally

Cons

- Possible fatigue and burnout before the exam
- You could find it hard to retain all you have learned
- A hiatus between taking the course and taking the exam

finishing the course and taking the bar exam. If so, you may want to take the early exam preparation course in your penultimate term. Alternatively, you may prefer having the momentum of the early preparation course behind you as you roll into the final exam preparation period after graduation. In that case, taking the early preparation course in the ultimate term is the way to go.

ELECTIVE COURSES

Depending on the law school, early bar preparation courses may be mandatory or elective. If your law school does not require a preparation course for the bar exam, you will need to evaluate several factors before deciding whether the elective course is right for you. Consider, for example:

★ Your performance quality during law school, in courses that are tested on the bar exam.

★ Your comfort level with particular exam question formats (for example, essay exams, performance tests, multiple-choice questions, and so on).

★ Your demonstrated level of exam anxiety. More familiarity with the bar exam may calm the related anxiety.

★ Whether you took the courses for the subjects tested on the bar exam while you were in law school.

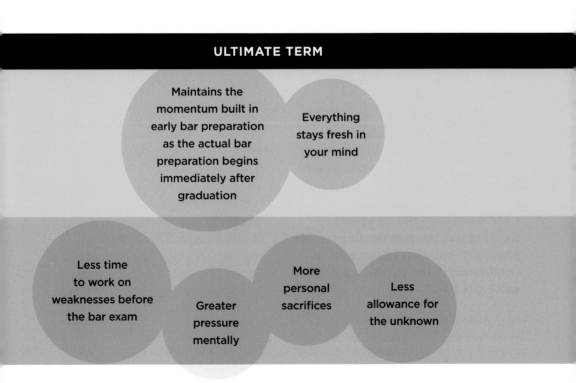

ULTIMATE TERM

Maintains the momentum built in early bar preparation as the actual bar preparation begins immediately after graduation

Everything stays fresh in your mind

Less time to work on weaknesses before the bar exam

Greater pressure mentally

More personal sacrifices

Less allowance for the unknown

GRADUATION REQUIREMENTS

Many law schools have requirements for graduation beyond grade point averages and course completion. Each law school, for example, has a certain number of units or credits that must be completed before you can graduate. Failing to complete all graduation requirements in a timely manner may cause your graduation and bar exam dates to be delayed.

PROVEN WRITING ABILITY

You may be required to demonstrate your professional writing ability by researching and writing a substantial paper. Many law schools have an upper-level writing requirement that may be satisfied through a seminar course with a substantial paper or an independent research paper that is supervised by a faculty member. Law schools have varying page or word and citation requirements and there may be several stages of writing involved. Check with your registrar or advisor for your school's requirements. See also Chapter Five: Legal Research and Writing Beyond the First Year.

"When you see something like bad writing, the first thing you think is, 'Well, if he didn't have enough time to spend writing it well, how much time did he spend researching it? How much time did he spend thinking out the ramifications of his position?' You don't have a lot of confidence in the substance if the writing is bad."

United States Supreme Court Justice
John G. Roberts

WORK EXPERIENCE

Another potential requirement for graduation is taking a course during which you get actual experience working with a licensed attorney. These courses are called "experiential" courses and most law schools have a requirement for at least three units. The experiential unit requirement may be satisfied by live client clinics, simulation courses, or externships. Check with your school to see what its requirements are for experiential learning. See also Part 4: Career and Professional Development.

UNIT CHECKS

The commencement of your final year in law school is a good time to do a unit/credit check to make sure you are on track to meet your graduation requirements. Schedule an appointment with your faculty advisor and the registrar to go over the graduation requirements. Registrar offices generally have a checklist of all requirements, including fees and deadlines associated with some requirements. Getting an early start on your graduation/unit check is essential to completing law school on time and staying on track for the bar exam.

BAR EXAM APPLICATIONS

Every jurisdiction that is responsible for licensing attorneys has its own application process for the bar exam. This process may include more than one application. For example, most jurisdictions in the United States require an application to take the exam, one to type the exam on a laptop, another to receive a testing accommodation, or even to wear religious headgear. Be sure to check your jurisdiction's website for the eligibility requirements for sitting the bar exam, and the fees and deadlines for each application.

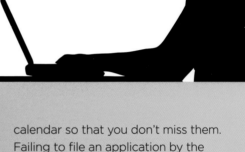

SUBMITTING YOUR APPLICATION

The licensing process will include the payment of fees and very strict deadlines for submitting the application to take the exam that occurs at the same time for each exam cycle. Put these dates on your calendar so that you don't miss them. Failing to file an application by the deadline can result in hefty late fees, or not being able to take the exam at all for that exam cycle.

Pro tips

BE PREPARED

If you have a learning disability and intend to apply for an accommodation, gather information about past diagnoses and treatment in preparation for your accommodation petition when making your bar exam application. If you have never been diagnosed, it is likely you will need to be tested.

MORAL CHARACTER

Lawyers are officers of the court and they must take an oath to uphold the laws and adhere to the professional ethics code for lawyers. Licensing agencies are tasked with protecting both the public and the profession from lawyers who demonstrate poor moral character. In addition to the bar exam application, most jurisdictions require applicants to complete an extensive background check and gain approval of their moral character either before sitting for the exam, or before being sworn in as a licensed member of the practicing bar.

COMPLETING YOUR APPLICATION

The moral character application is extensive and requires applicants to go back years to retrieve information that can be difficult to find. A good time to start this application is in the beginning of your final year in law school. Before you begin your moral character application, make sure you review the actual application so that you can begin collecting the information early.

THE CANDID APPLICANT

The most important thing to remember when completing the moral character application is to be completely candid and thorough. Review your application to law school for inconsistencies and repair the record by filing an amendment to your law school application as soon as possible. The registrar or recordkeeper of the law school should be able to explain the process of amending your law school application.

THE TIMELY APPLICANT

Completing your moral character application can take a while, depending upon your age and life experience. Once your application is submitted, it can take months to receive the notice of approval from the licensing agency. In jurisdictions that allow you to sit for the exam before your moral character application is approved, you could conceivably pass the exam, and not be eligible to be sworn in and practice law because you have not received approval of your moral character application. Start early, keep records, and update your moral character application after you submit it if information that you reported changes.

Pro tips

KEEP RECORDS

It's never too early to prepare for your moral character application before your memory gets stale. Gather hard-to-obtain information such as old traffic tickets, civil court cases, brushes with the law as a juvenile, details of past employers and supervisors. Doing this as an ongoing exercise reduces the risk of something getting overlooked.

YOUR MORAL CHARACTER

Here is a list of things you may be asked to disclose:

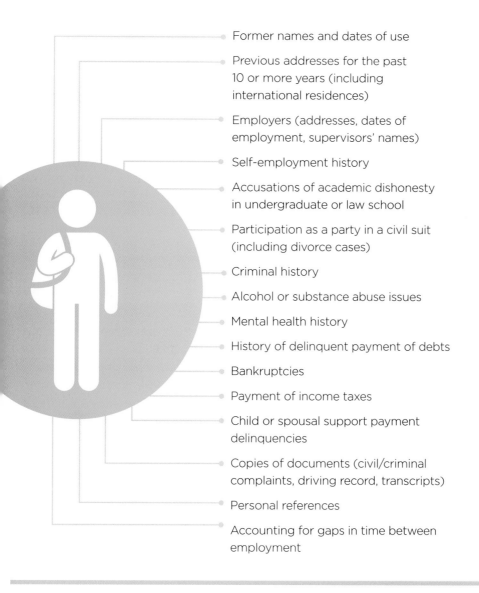

- Former names and dates of use
- Previous addresses for the past 10 or more years (including international residences)
- Employers (addresses, dates of employment, supervisors' names)
- Self-employment history
- Accusations of academic dishonesty in undergraduate or law school
- Participation as a party in a civil suit (including divorce cases)
- Criminal history
- Alcohol or substance abuse issues
- Mental health history
- History of delinquent payment of debts
- Bankruptcies
- Payment of income taxes
- Child or spousal support payment delinquencies
- Copies of documents (civil/criminal complaints, driving record, transcripts)
- Personal references
- Accounting for gaps in time between employment

"Laws control the lesser man. Right conduct controls the greater one."

Mark Twain, American author

YOUR FINANCES

Preparing for the bar exam is expensive! All of the applications for the exam have associated fees that, in the aggregate, can be more than US$1,000. In addition to the licensing and exam fees, commercial exam preparation courses or tutors can cost thousands. Add to that the cost of living while you are studying full-time for the exam, and you will see that preparing for your license is not cheap!

PREPARING A BUDGET

To ease the pain of financing your exam preparation period, begin planning your finances as early as the first year of law school. If possible, you should plan not to work during the preparation period because you will have a massive amount of information to review or learn for the first time. Your exam preparation could be as long as 12 hours per day, 5 to 7 days per week. Creating a budget for exam preparation time will ease the anxiety caused by having work time compete with crucial study time (see opposite). See also pages 22–23: Financial Planning.

STUDENT LOANS AND SAVINGS

There are many ways to plan your savings for the expenses associated with your bar exam preparation period from the start of law school. If you are relying on student loans to pay for law school, you may want to factor in a portion of your budget each semester or term to be set aside for the exam preparation period. Just remember that this money will accrue interest and will eventually have to be paid back, so only borrow what you need.

If you are working while attending law school, add exam preparation to your savings goal. You may use a special-purpose savings account that restricts your ability to withdraw those funds until a certain date. Special-purpose accounts earn interest so your savings can grow over time. Certain investment tools such as a Certificate of Deposit (CD) can also be used to save over a longer period of time.

BAR LOANS

Some private lending companies offer "bar loans" to help students pay for examination fees and living expenses. Bar loans from private lenders usually have a limit on how much you can borrow and allow you to get access to the money within 12 months of graduation. These loans are not part of the federal student loan program and are not eligible for deferrals, forbearances, or loan forgiveness programs that may be offered by government-backed loans. Additionally, the interest rates for these loans are often higher than government loans and may require you to have a cosigner or guarantor. Use caution and do your research if you plan to use private bar loans.

Sample budget

This sample budget lists exam and preparation course fees, plus living expenses for a 10-week study period. Of course, you may also have additional expenses to factor in, such as childcare or medical bills.

Expense	Amount USD (approx.)
Bar exam application fee	$560.00
Moral character application fee	$680.00
Registration for the bar exam fee	$155.00
Laptop use fee	$120.00
Multistate professional responsibility exam	$190.00
Exam preparation course	$4,000.00
Housing for three months	$6,000.00
Utilities for three months	$600.00
Food for three months	$900.00
Car note and insurance for three months	$1,500.00
Smartphone for three months	$240.00
Total	$14,945.00

STUDY TIME

Preparing for your licensing exam is time- and life-consuming. During a relatively brief period after law school, you will embark on an intense review and study journey that will require thousands of pages of reading, dozens of hours of lectures, and potentially thousands of practice exam questions to complete and review.

It is not uncommon in some jurisdictions, for students to spend 10 to 12 hours each day, 5 to 7 days each week, for 10 weeks studying for this exam. Needless to say, time is a valuable commodity during the exam preparation period. Working out how you will be able to get this time is very important. See also pages 92–93: Planning Your Time.

SAVING VACATION TIME

Many people secure their exam preparation time by saving vacation time from work. If you are able to bank vacation time, start early. This will ensure that you can still receive your pay while you are studying and can reduce the amount of money you

may need to borrow and repay. Some employers cap the amount of time you can accrue for vacation. If your earned vacation time exceeds that amount, you may lose the excess time. Talk to your employer about how much vacation time you can accrue.

CREATIVE WORK SCHEDULES

As good as it sounds to be able to take time off work to focus solely on your bar exam preparation, not all students have that luxury. If you must work during the exam preparation period, speak to your employer early about creative work schedules that can accommodate your studies. You will still need to study during nonwork hours, but you may be able to gain more time by creating an alternative work schedule. Here are a few suggestions:

★ If you can afford it, take an unpaid leave of absence.
★ Take one full day off each week and make up the time either before or after exam preparation.
★ Reduce work hours during the exam preparation period.
★ Change your work shift so that your most productive study time is during the time when you will take the exam.

Pro tips

ALLOCATE YOUR LEISURE TIME

Be sure to spread your time off over the entire course of your exam preparation period to avoid cramming in the final few weeks before the exam.

FAMILY SUPPORT

A supportive family, even when it comes to the little things, can make a very positive difference to the quality of your exam preparation. However, "support" may mean different things to different people, so it is important to consider what sort of contributions would be most helpful to you, and then to provide your support network with clear requests in advance of your studies.

"In every conceivable manner, the family is a link to our past, bridge to our future."

Alex Haley, American author

MORAL SUPPORT

Exam preparation can be exhausting and stressful. A positive affirmation or words of encouragement can go a long way. Ask your support network to send positive messages from time to time to help you through the rough periods.

CHILDCARE

If you have small children, try to arrange childcare before your exam preparation begins. It is important to have uninterrupted, focused study time so that you can absorb the information and complete timed practice exams.

HOUSEHOLD CHORES

Of course, you don't get to shirk ALL of your responsibilities, but you may be able to avoid a few. In aggregate, laundry, dishes, yard work, and so on, can eat away at your precious study time, so recruit some help.

FOOD PREPARATION

Little things like prepping nutritous, homemade meals can really add up in terms of time. Cooking in bulk can both increase available study time, plus ensure that you stay healthy during exam prep. Enlist the help of family and friends for at least one meal a day.

CHAPTER SEVEN

TAKING THE BAR EXAM

Well, here you are in the final stretch of your law school journey! You have laid your professional foundation through your discovery and mastery of the law and developed skills to demonstrate that mastery. All that you have accomplished over the past three years has led you to this point, and all that is left to do before you are a licensed attorney is to pass one more exam.

While your license is the icing on the cake, the cake itself is the transformation that you have gone through to become a highly skilled critical thinker, problem-solver, and analytical writer. Now it's time to show your stuff!

In the previous chapter, you learned how law school exams are different from the bar (licensing) exams that serve as your entry into the practice of law. Still, your legal education plays a critical role in providing a strong foundation for both the bar exam and the practice of law. Mastering essential knowledge and skills during law school and developing a strong discipline for studying will put you in a good position to pass your exam on the first attempt.

In most places, you must pass a comprehensive and intense bar exam if you want to practice law. The bar exam is a high stakes affair that carries with it immense pressure, emotion, fear, and anxiety for many students. A strong foundation from law school is essential to your preparation for this exam. This chapter will broadly discuss the intersection between law school and the bar exam, the structure and content of U.S. bar exams, commercial bar review companies, and the process of bar preparation. The ultimate goal in taking the bar exam is to pass it the first time, so take it seriously.

YOUR LAW SCHOOL FOUNDATION

One of the most enduring myths about legal education is that people go to law school to learn "the law." It is called "law" school, after all! But in reality, the purpose of law school is not to learn the law, rather it is to understand legal principles and to develop the skills necessary to "learn" the law and how to use it to advocate for your clients. It is an absolute impossibility to learn everything there is to know about the law and retain it in your head. Besides, laws change, laws get repealed, and when new issues emerge in our society, new laws are born.

MASTERING LEGAL PRINCIPLES

There are basic principles that underlie every substantive area of law from which a deeper understanding of rules and policy emerge. For example, reading court opinions and understanding how the law developed and how the facts of the case led the court to its resolution of the parties' issues is the primary method of mastering legal principles over time. It is not about memorizing specific rules. "Principles" run deep and pop up in several subjects. For example, the legal theory of "objectiveness" is the basis for contract formation, criminal conspiracies, negligence, and constitutional protections against self-incrimination. Law school is the time and place to master these legal principles.

ANALYTICAL AND ADVOCACY SKILLS

In addition to teaching you how to understand legal principles, law school will help you develop analytical and advocacy skills so that you can use the law to serve your clients. This is done largely through reading and briefing court opinions, through Socratic discussions in class, and through cocurricular activities such as moot court, mock trial, and alternative dispute resolution team competitions. This combination of understanding legal principles and developing analytical and advocacy skills to deploy your knowledge is the foundation you must have to begin your bar exam preparation. Without it, you will be running the impossible race of trying to learn and develop these things in the short period of time leading up to the exam. See also Chapter Five: Legal Research and Writing Beyond the First Year and pages 100–101: The Litigation Attorney.

DOS AND DON'TS

Do look for connections between legal principles across subjects in law school. The importance of these connections will become truly apparent as you review multiple subjects in preparation for your bar exam.

Don't be lured by the false promises of commercial briefs or rote memorization of legal terms. Read and brief all of your cases throughout law school. The more you read and brief, the better and faster you become at recognizing and solving legal issues.

EXAM-TAKING SKILLS

There are only two times in your legal career that you will ever need to take an essay exam or multiple-choice exam: at law school and in the bar exam. Consequently, mastering exam-taking skills in these two formats while you are in law school makes passing the ultimate exam that much easier. While practicing law does not require you to answer exam questions, it does require you to solve problems.

Practice, practice, practice exam skills! Lawyers solve problems. It's what we do. Like most things in life, if you want to be good at something, you need to practice it . . . a lot! Exam-taking skills are no different. Think about it. Exams are basically a set of hypothetical problems that you, as the examinee, must solve. Whether the question format requires an essay, short answers, or multiple-choice answers, all law school exams embody legal problems. In law school, make practice exams an integral part of your study and exam preparation process so that when you are in the throes of preparing for your bar exam, you will not have to build these skills from scratch.

> **"Practice makes perfect. After a long time of practicing our work will become natural, skillful, swift, and steady."**

Bruce Lee, martial artist and actor

BAR EXAMS: STRUCTURE AND CONTENT

The bar exam measures minimal competency to practice law and has the stated purpose of protecting the public from incompetent attorneys. It is the primary vehicle by which people gain access to the practicing bar. For the most part, the bar exam is drafted in part by the National Conference of Bar Examiners (NCBE) and in part by individual states or territories. In the United States and its territories, the bar exam is administered twice a year at the end of February and July, and each jurisdiction sets its own passing score and other eligibility requirements.

COMPOSITION

The exam generally includes two to three components, depending on the jurisdiction. All jurisdictions use the essay format as part of the bar exam, and all but one state (Louisiana) and one territory (Puerto Rico) use the Multistate Bar Exam (MBE). About 85% of the U.S. jurisdictions use some form of performance test.

ESSAY EXAM

Every U.S. jurisdiction uses the essay format on the bar exam, which is administered around the same time as the MBE. Jurisdictions vary in terms of the law that is tested, the number of essay questions, and the time allotted to each essay. In addition to the MBE, the NCBE also drafts essay questions (Multistate Essay Exams or MEE) for some jurisdictions. The MEE essays do not cover state-specific law but focus instead on federal common and statutory law. A few states and Puerto Rico draft their own essays that use a mixture of federal common and statutory law and state-specific law. The number of essays on a bar exam may range from 3 to 15 depending on the jurisdiction.

MULTISTATE BAR EXAM

The Multistate Bar Exam (MBE) is a six-hour, 200-question, multiple-choice test. The MBE is always administered on the same day, with all jurisdictions taking it at the same time. The exam tests a mixture of common law and federal constitutional and statutory law over eight subjects (see right).

★ Federal civil procedure

★ Federal constitutional law

★ Contracts law (including the common law and the Uniform Commercial Code)

★ Criminal law

★ Federal criminal procedure

★ Federal rules of evidence

★ Real property law

★ Torts law

Note: While criminal law and federal criminal procedure are separate areas of law, they are tested together on the MBE.

PERFORMANCE TEST

The performance test has gained popularity in the United States over the past two decades. Currently, 49 U.S. jurisdictions use either a multistate performance test, or a performance test drafted by the individual jurisdiction. The performance test is a "closed universe problem" that includes a hypothetical client file and a library that contains law from a fictitious jurisdiction. Examinees are given a set of instructions by a supervising attorney, in the form of a task memo and must produce a document that demonstrates their ability to manage a case and think and write like a lawyer.

BAR REVIEW COURSES

After graduation from law school, it is common for those about to embark on the final stage of preparation for the bar exam, to purchase a commercial bar review course to aid them. Commercial bar review companies offer a wide variety of courses and materials for those studying for the bar exam, including subject-matter outlines, live or video lectures, and a combination of released and company-drafted practice questions in each exam format.

Bar review companies are proprietary, and their materials are generally tailored to meet the exam requirements of each jurisdiction. These commercial bar review courses can be very expensive, ranging from hundreds to thousands of dollars. Law schools and bar review companies often partner together in order to provide students a discounted course.

Choosing a course

Not all bar review courses are equal. Here are a few things to look for when choosing a course:

★ Length of time in business and reputation

★ Number of practice MBEs available. (Ideally you should have access to over 2,000 MBE questions with answer explanations.)

★ Quality of the answer explanations for the MBE questions

★ Online performance tracking and analysis with automatic remediation of weaker topics

★ Number of state-released essay and performance exams with sample answers

★ Quality of the subject matter outlines. The multistate subject outline should include all topics from the NCBE's subject matter outline for the MBE. Some outlines are sparser than others. A strong outline should include not only a full complement of rules, but also examples of how many of those rules get applied in a factual scenario.

★ Quality of video lectures

★ Cost

★ Whether you can repeat the course for free if necessary

★ Whether you receive graded feedback on your essays or performance tests

Many law schools invite bar review companies to their campus to showcase and sell their programs. Spend time looking through the materials. Ask questions about additional support that may be available during law school or the post-law school bar exam preparation period. Most of these companies offer heavily discounted or free courses to student representatives who recruit fellow students to a bar review course. Acting as a student sales representative is a great way to trim the budget for bar preparation!

PRIVATE TUTORS

Some students feel more at ease with a private tutor than with a larger, more generic bar review program. A private tutor may be more expensive than a formal bar review course and it may be harder to establish the strength of a tutor's reputation for helping students pass the bar exam, so try to get recommendations from people you know and trust. Some private tutors do not have the quantity or quality of review materials that a commercial bar review company might have. There is also a chance that they will create their own materials, which may or may not be developed carefully or accurately. When deciding on a private tutor, consider the following:

★ The tutor's years of experience and success rate
★ The scope of work (for example, number of meetings, essay and performance test feedback and review, and so on)
★ The cost
★ Free or discounted subsequent tutoring if you have to take the bar again
★ Whether you have to pay extra to receive materials

Be wary of private tutors who offer "short cuts" and tricks to passing the bar exam or profess to make predictions about what subjects will be tested. Only hard work and persistence will win the day.

PLANNING YOUR TIME

Like law school, bar preparation is an immersive process that touches many areas in your life, both personally and professionally. To have a successful bar preparation experience, build on the lessons you learned in Chapter Six by creating a strong, comprehensive, yet detailed plan that includes study and your general life activities. The implementation of your plan will require self-regulation, discipline, persistence, and balance.

WORKING TO A PLAN

Taking a commercial bar review course after graduation is not required, but is strongly advised. These courses are designed specifically for the bar exam in your jurisdiction and are generally kept up-to-date in terms of recent changes to the law and the actual exam topics. If you are taking a commercial bar review course, it will likely include a detailed plan or schedule of work for you to do over an 8-to-10-week period before the bar exam. These schedules tend to be generic, with a one-size-fits-all approach, but some bar review companies have partnerships with law schools and are able to tailor the schedule and program to the needs of those particular students. See also pages 90–91: Bar Review Courses.

TAILORING YOUR PLAN

Depending on your needs, you may need to customize your bar review course study schedule to address time constraints created by your religious practices, job and family responsibilities, knowledge readiness in particular subject areas, and strengths and weaknesses in the different exam formats. In any case, you must consider that the schedule provided by your bar review course offers you a baseline of work to complete. You may need to spend more than the recommended amount of time and do more work than is set out in the schedule. You will need to adjust your plan over time as you begin to understand the routine of bar exam preparation.

"Persistence is the quality of winners. Successful people never give up."

Lynda Field, motivational speaker and life coach

SELF-REGULATION

Bar exam preparation is an individual experience. While there will be activities that are suitable for groups, such as watching video lectures and doing simulated exams, the vast majority of time is spent developing your understanding of the legal principles and sharpening your exam-taking skills. Each person in the bar exam preparation course will be at a different point in their journey, so you must focus on your own. There is much work to be done during bar review. Unlike law school, there will be no professors to take attendance, no one to check in on your progress, and no class discussions to shape your understanding of the law. You will need to regulate your own behavior and be accountable for completing assignments in a timely manner.

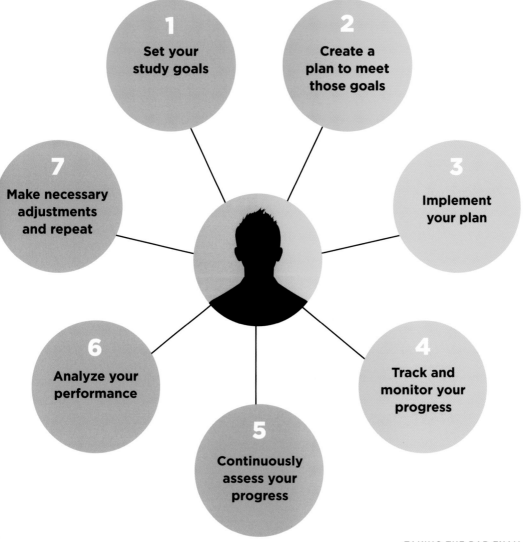

1 Set your study goals

2 Create a plan to meet those goals

3 Implement your plan

4 Track and monitor your progress

5 Continuously assess your progress

6 Analyze your performance

7 Make necessary adjustments and repeat

DISCIPLINE AND PERSISTENCE

Consistent, focused, methodical progress is essential to success on the bar exam. Reading, watching lectures, doing countless practice questions and getting more of them wrong than you thought was possible can begin to wear you down. This is the point at which discipline and persistence can save the day, and your bar preparation.

🚫 LEARN TO SAY "NO"

Your life must fit into bar preparation, not the other way around, so you have to learn to say "no" to extra demands placed on your time. You may need to decline invitations to destination weddings, family vacations, and other tempting activities that will cut into your precious time. To the extent possible, ask family and friends to be conscious of scheduling major events during your bar study time, if they expect you to attend.

⚖️ FIND BALANCE

With intense bar exam preparation, it is easy to fall out of alignment with life. Days can begin to run together and all you can see is the mountain of work ahead. Creating balance in your day is critical to avoid becoming overwhelmed. Discipline and balance go hand in hand. Stick to your schedule so that you complete your assigned study tasks within the given amount of time. Then, when study time is over, plan relaxing and rejuvenating activities to balance out your day.

🪷 PRESERVE YOUR MENTAL HEALTH

Make time in your day to take short breaks so you can clear your mind. Mindfulness meditation is a great way to begin and end your days and inject a little peace in the middle. Maintaining established exercise routines or beginning a light routine of walking or yoga does wonders for your mental health and focus. See also Chapter Fifteen: Taking Care of Yourself.

Once the bar exam is over, you should consider taking a vacation to recover from the long and arduous study period. It may seem very strange that you have no essay questions to write and no MBE questions to practice. Give yourself time to come back to normal, it's been a very long road!

🏠 CONTINUED SUPPORT

Your bar review schedule provides the roadmap to follow through bar preparation, but you might need to push yourself past some of the more challenging points along the way. Family and friends who have not been through the law school and bar exam experience may think that your journey is done. After all, the bar exam is just another test and you've already passed so many! You may need to educate your support group about how support required during the runup to the bar exam is different than during law school. Explain to them that you will have less time to spend with them or to do chores around the house, not more than you had in law school.

WHAT YOU HAVE TIME FOR

Here are just a few important differences between your life during law school and your life during bar preparation.

During School	**During Bar Preparation**
Light schoolwork on the weekends so more social time.	Eight to twelve hours of studying one or both days of the weekend.
Time to work part-time around your school schedule.	Such an intense study load that many students simply cannot continue with employment.
Making time for family vacations, weddings, and other social functions.	Need to be very selective about which social events to attend, if any.

Pro tips

TIPS FOR STAYING ON TRACK

★ Check your bar preparation schedule for the next day before you go to bed each night.

★ At a minimum, finish everything on your schedule each day so you don't get behind.

★ Don't be a box-checker! Do more, not less, if you want to get better.

★ Keep track of the subjects you are doing well in and those subjects where you are weak. Focus your extra time on the weaker subjects.

★ Don't study linearly (one subject then another). Rotate your practice in the subjects each week so you never lose ground in any particular subject.

CHAPTER EIGHT

AFTER THE RACE: WHERE TO GO FROM HERE

Thanks to your hard work over the last three years, you now hold one of the most powerful and versatile advanced degrees in the world. Think of the magnitude of that accomplishment! There are many examples of notable trial lawyers and learned legal scholars and justices, but you might be surprised to discover how many actors, athletes, CEO's, musicians, and medical doctors have, like you, earned a law degree.

In nearly every waking moment of our lives we bump up against law. Whether dealing with professional or personal problems, the problem-solving skills you developed as part of your legal training are priceless. Now that the bar exam is over, it's time to figure out how you can put that law degree to work for you!

Do you want to practice criminal law or civil law? Do you want to be a domestic relations lawyer or a state or federal legislative aide? What if you are not even certain that you want to practice law at all? If you do not already know what you want to do with your Juris Doctor (JD) degree, don't worry. Your legal education will expose you to the breadth and depth of the legal profession, including a plethora of legal practice areas. There are many avenues to explore and many choices to make.

Your path through law school may take unexpected turns as you become more familiar with the profession. This chapter discusses the three major classes of attorneys (transactional, litigation, and appellate), the courses in law school that help prepare you for careers in those classes, and how you can use the opportunities provided by your law school to help shape and define your career. The good news is, you don't have to decide your practice area or type of practice now. Use your experiences in law school and the resources it provides, to guide you to your best career.

THE TRANSACTIONAL ATTORNEY

Not all attorneys are drawn to the high drama of the courtroom stage that you often see played out on television. Some prefer the quiet, strategic planning and implementation that goes into resolving potential issues for their clients. The transactional attorney's work starts at the beginning of a legal issue, before a lawsuit is ever conceived of or filed. These attorneys are masters at anticipation, creation, and preservation.

THE ROLE

Transactional attorneys bring people together, preserve relationships, and build and protect businesses with the ultimate goal of avoiding the dreaded, yet sometimes necessary, litigation that results when disputes cannot be resolved amicably. They accomplish the goal of litigation avoidance by becoming expert researchers, negotiators, constructionists, and drafters of documents and agreements that can withstand most legal challenges. While some attorneys do both transaction and litigation work, it is not uncommon for them to focus on only one or the other. Many transactional attorneys choose this route because it is generally less stressful and thus more conducive to work-life balance than litigation work, which tends to be more like a rollercoaster ride at times.

PRACTICE AREAS

The practice areas for transactional law are vast. Transactional attorneys draft wills and trusts and they structure and manage the acquisition of corporations or corporate assets. They draft contracts

Typical transactions courses

There are generally far more courses in law school that are transactional in nature than there are litigation courses. They include:

★ Business organizations

★ Nonprofit corporation law

★ Contracts (including sales contracts under the Uniform Commercial Code UCC)

★ Trusts and decedent estates

★ Real estate transactions

★ Secured transactions

★ Patent law

★ Family law (prenuptial agreements)

★ Environmental law

★ Oil and gas law

and leases, or prepare and file patent or trademark applications, orchestrate class-action lawsuits, and conduct nearly any other preparatory or compliance work for private and public entities.

Pro tips

BROADEN YOUR EXPERIENCE

If your interests lie in transactional law, it is still a good idea to take some litigation courses and maybe even do an externship in a litigation unit. Knowing what is likely to happen if a transaction ends in litigation can help inform additional protections to include in a document during the drafting process. A good transactional attorney should be able to anticipate how the documents they draft, or the business structures they build, will hold up in a court of law or equity.

THE TRANSACTIONAL ATTORNEY'S SKILL SET

While all attorneys must acquire general practice skills, the transactional attorney benefits from developing a specific skill set. For a career as a transactional attorney, you should aim to master the following skills in law school:

- ☑ Research
- ☑ Critical reading
- ☑ Oral and written communication
- ☑ Analytical writing
- ☑ Negotiation
- ☑ Statutory and regulatory interpretation
- ☑ Organizational

THE LITIGATION ATTORNEY

Litigation attorneys are masters of the judicial process. They are the attorneys most often popularized in courtroom dramas on television and in movies. In short, litigators try cases in court playing to an audience of one or more people who will help resolve the dispute. Some of these litigators try criminal cases and some litigate broadly in the area of civil law. Regardless of whether the practice is criminal or civil, litigators do the important work of advocating for their clients in court.

THE ROLE

While litigators are the most popular class of attorneys, interestingly, the vast majority of lawsuits do not end in a trial. Cases are most often settled in the pretrial phase at various points in the legal process. Nevertheless litigation attorneys need to be familiar with core principles regarding the legal process such as 1) how to file a civil lawsuit, 2) the requirements for a search warrant, or 3) what evidence is likely to be admitted during trial if one actually occurs. If being a litigator is high on your list of career goals, check with your law school to see a full list of available litigation courses and supporting extracurricular activities that can help you build a strong foundation for a career.

COMPETITIONS

Cocurricular competition teams such as moot court, mock trial, and alternative dispute resolution teams offer students exciting practical experiences before a panel of professors, lawyers, or actual judges. Competition teams can be conducted intraschool, regionally, nationally, or internationally and are sponsored by a variety of organizations. They can include

Typical litigation courses

There are a number of courses in law school where you can explore the litigation field. They include:

★ Procedural courses such as civil or criminal procedure

★ Evidence

★ Litigation-simulation courses such as trial advocacy

broad substantive practice areas or be targeted to specific areas such as civil rights law. These competitions allow students to demonstrate both their written and oral advocacy skills and earn trophies and placement among their peers at other law schools. Outstanding performance in a competition looks very impressive on a resume for that first job out of law school.

INTERNSHIP PROGRAMS

Many jurisdictions have some sort of certified legal internship program that allows law students in good standing to practice law before a court, under the close supervision of a licensed attorney. Detailed information about the eligibility requirements for such programs can often be found online. For students interested in public interest law, city, county, state, and federal prosecutors and public defenders offices offer externships to provide students with the opportunity to work with real clients under the close supervision of a licensed attorney. See also Chapter Twelve: Internships and Externships.

THE LITIGATION ATTORNEY'S SKILL SET

For a career as a litigation attorney, you should aim to master the following skills in law school:

- ☑ Strong oral advocacy
- ☑ Keen listening
- ☑ Quick critical thinking
- ☑ Good negotiation
- ☑ Organization
- ☑ Time management

"My client may deserve serious punishment, but first prove that's the case. And remember at all times that he's a human being, which means he must be treated with minimum standards of decency because doing so redeems not only him but you."

Scott Turow Lincoln, American lawyer and author

THE APPELLATE ATTORNEY

After all of the transactional and litigation work is complete, cases will often be appealed to the next highest court or court of appeals. Clients who lost at the pretrial or trial level get a second chance to prevail in their cases on appeal. Appellate attorneys can be thought of as fixers. Generally, they swoop in after a case has been decided already and try to persuade the appeal court that the trial court should have decided the case differently.

THE ROLE

Attorneys who practice appellate work review and analyze the trial court record, research and write persuasive briefs, and advocate for their clients before the appellate court. Some appellate attorneys work closely with the litigators on a case before or during trial to help them frame the case in a way that will aid the appeal if one is needed. See also page 64: Advanced Appellate Advocacy.

COCURRICULAR ACTIVITIES

For cocurricular activities geared toward appellate practice, you should try to earn a spot on your school's law review or another significant journal. Participation on a journal's editorial board strengthens your research and writing skills. Also, seek out judicial internships at the trial or appeal court levels. In addition to gaining tremendous insight and experience in this area, adding a coveted judicial clerkship to your resume can make you more attractive to appellate law firms after law school. If your goal is to ultimately be a judge, a judicial clerkship is a good way to go. See also pages 68–69: Scholarly Writing.

Typical appellate law courses

The law school courses that support a career in appellate law are similar to courses that are helpful for transactional and litigation law; however, there are also courses that are specific to appellate law.

★ Appellate advocacy

★ Federal courts

★ Advanced legal research

★ Advanced legal writing

★ Law review

★ Constitutional law

★ Appellate procedure

DO YOUR RESEARCH

1. When researching law schools, check out the number of judicial internships awarded to students at each school.

2. Research the top appellate attorney firms to see which law schools they hire most of their attorneys from.

3. Look at which law schools boast the highest number of appeal court judges.

THE APPELLATE ATTORNEY'S SKILL SET

For a career as an appellate attorney, you should aim to master the following skills in law school:

☑ Critical reading

☑ Critical thinking

☑ Researching

☑ Persuasive writing

☑ Oral advocacy

☑ A very strong understanding of legal principles and procedure for appellate practice

CHOOSING SIDES

In addition to the three major classes of attorneys, most attorneys will focus their practice on either plaintiff work or defense work. Plaintiff-side attorneys bring civil lawsuits on behalf of their clients who they feel have been wrongfully harmed. Defense-side attorneys work to protect the person or entity being sued or charged with a crime. This choice of whether to work as a plaintiff-side or defense-side attorney is often guided by one's social, political, or economic views, so attorneys tend to be fiercely loyal to their chosen side.

PAYMENT STRUCTURES

From a practical standpoint, there are some other significant differences between plaintiff and defense attorneys. One big difference is the way clients pay for services. The ability of the person being sued (defendant) to pay a monetary award is a key factor in deciding whether to sue them at all. After all, why spend the time and energy suing someone if they have no money to pay the judgment?

Payment structure for a defense attorney

$		$	
Sign Retainer Agreement	Begin work Respond to pleadings Conduct discovery	Bill for work	Conduct interviews Draft responses Attend hearings

Payment structure for a plaintiff attorney

Sign Agreement	Meet with client Meet with witnesses File complaint	Work	Conduct discovery File motions Attend hearings

Defense attorneys normally bill a fixed amount or an hourly rate that is set out in a retainer agreement. Since defense work, by its nature, is responsive to a plaintiff's lawsuit, the amount of time spent on research, responding to correspondence from the plaintiff's attorney, and appearing at court hearings, and so on, is billed as it occurs, so defense attorneys are usually paid in advance or as the case proceeds through the judicial process.

The payment structure for a plaintiff's attorney depends largely on the strength of the case and the client's ability to pay up front or during the case. If a plaintiff has a strong case with a good likelihood of winning a substantial award in court or settling the case before court, the attorney may take the case on contingency. This usually means that the plaintiff does not have to pay his or her attorney's fees unless or until they win the case. Of course, this is risky for the attorney because a case may take several months to several years to develop and conclude. If the outcome is not favorable, the attorney does not get paid for the work they have done. Consequently, plaintiff-side attorneys take of lot of care to evaluate cases before agreeing to handle them. If the attorney's assessment of the case is validated by winning, the fee is usually 25% to 33% of the award, depending on whether the case settled before trial or the client won at trial. The more time the case takes, the higher the percentage of the award is for the attorney's fee. Cases where the award is in the millions, or even billions, can definitely be worth the wait both from a justice and a monetary perspective.

Bill for work

**Prepare for trial
Negotiate settlement
Wrap up case**

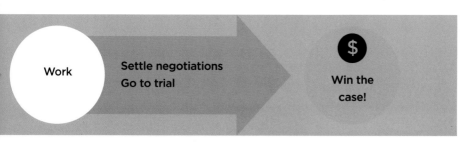

Work

**Settle negotiations
Go to trial**

Win the case!

A NONLEGAL CAREER

Not everyone who attends law school has the desire to take a bar exam and practice law. You might wonder why anyone would go through the toils of law school if they did not actually want to practice. In fact, the power of a JD degree is underestimated in nonlegal careers. This may be a result of the myth that people go to law school to learn the law. The critical thinking, analytical, and communication skills that are the hallmarks of a good legal education translate to nearly any career field, legal or nonlegal.

LAW IN EVERYDAY LIFE

It's hard to conceive of something we do on a daily basis that is not governed by or impacted by law. As members of society, even when we are not at work, we are impacted by law. When you buy a package of meat at the grocery store, the law of sales governs your purchase. When you buy a ticket from the movie theater, you are a party to a contract. If you are involved in a traffic accident, someone likely violated a law and is liable for civil or criminal penalties. If you own a dog, there are laws that regulate how your dog must present in public (leash laws) and what your responsibility is if your dog bites someone.

SELF-EMPLOYED WITH A JD DEGREE

Whether you work in the public or private sector, you will run up against law the moment your day begins. If you have your own business, having a good general understanding of the law that impacts your business is invaluable. As a restaurant owner, for example, your ability to draft and review contracts with your vendors can be a first layer of protection for you. Understanding premise liability law helps you put safety measures in place to protect your business from lawsuits if a customer is injured by a condition on your property. Understanding the basic principles of property law can make you be a more astute negotiator when purchasing or leasing the building for your restaurant. The list goes on! Having a law degree does not mean that your business will never need to hire another attorney, but it can significantly limit your exposure to liability before an incident occurs.

Potential JD-advantage careers

★ Ethics and compliance

★ Contract procurement and compliance

★ Patent and trademark procurement

★ Government or community relations

★ Transportation and shipping

★ Equity and inclusion officer

★ Real estate management

★ Technology licensing

★ Foreign service

★ Construction management

★ Sports and entertainment

★ Nonprofit management

★ Higher education and K-12

★ Military

★ The medical profession

★ Risk management

EMPLOYEES WITH A JD DEGREE

Many employers benefit when high-level employees have a law degree. Companies with human resource departments recruiting for a director or vice president position may include a JD as a preferred degree due to job duties such as managing labor relations, handling discrimination complaints, or structuring compensation packages. A technology or engineering firm would benefit from a manager or leader who has a good grasp of privacy, patent, or trademark law. A candidate for a hospital administrator position who has legal insight into malpractice law or product liability law has an advantage over a candidate without such knowledge.

YOUR FUTURE

Whether you are looking for a career in law that requires a license to practice, or simply a career enhancement, a JD degree offers a lot of flexibility. Don't worry if it takes you some time to figure out exactly what you want to accomplish with your JD degree. Research your options before starting law school so that you are fully prepared to maximize your opportunity to have the career of your dreams, but don't be surprised if your dreams evolve. Keep your mind open to all of the amazing possibilities available to you.

"When you cross the finish line, no matter how slow or fast, it will change your life forever."

Dick Beardsley, American long-distance runner and motivational author

PART

CAREER AND PROFESSIONAL DEVELOPMENT

CHAPTER NINE

PROFESSIONAL IDENTITY

Congratulations! You're off and running, and your technique looks great! Now let's discuss the type of legal athlete you would like to become. You've heard of "sportsmanship"? Well, the same idea applies to law school and the legal profession. How you conduct yourself as a law student and as a lawyer is extremely important—you want to be remembered for your positive contributions.

Some students may have established the foundation of their identity in a previous career or through participation in various organizations before starting law school. In each new adventure, you can take advantage of the opportunity to reinvent yourself or to hone the skills and qualities that contribute to your character. The legal profession subscribes to a particular set of rules or a code of ethics. Your behavior outside the courtroom is just as important as your conduct inside the courtroom. The importance placed on civility is evident through various professional legal organizations such as the American Bar Association and local bar associations whose aim it is to preserve ethics and civility.

This chapter focuses on you and asks tough questions designed to assist you in establishing your professional identity. Examining yourself before the first day of law school, and being aware of your personal and professional evolution as you progress in your academic and professional career, arms you with the confidence you'll need when attending networking events, interviews, and even striking up conversations with strangers on public transit. Reading through this chapter will require you to stop and think and spend time on yourself. Take your time and provide thoughtful answers to the questions presented.

WHO ARE YOU AND WHY ARE YOU HERE?

Honest self-reflection should serve as a foundation to any important decision you make. Professors, employers, and law school advisors often ask law students "Who are you?," "What drives you?," and "Why are you here?" If you have not taken the time to answer these questions, here is some food for thought to help you reflect.

? From birth to the present day, think about your life experiences—big and small, important and seemingly unimportant. Note down anything that stands out to you, anything that may have led you to become the person you are today.

? Consider why you believe these experiences to be important and note that down as well. After some reflection, consider how these experiences are linked, and how they help define who you are, your character, your morals, and your motivation.

? Now that you have an idea of who you are, ask yourself, "Why am I here?" This question is pertinent; prospective employers will ask this, although it will sound more like, "So tell me, why did you go to law school?" Your ability to clearly and succinctly answer this question is crucial, as it shows that you have thoughtfully considered your degree and future career path.

? Now that you have a clearer idea of the direction of your professional identity, let's work on your message. In two to three sentences, explain why you are pursuing a legal career and what you hope to achieve with your degree and subsequent license.

Pro tips

ESTABLISHING YOUR PERSONAL BRAND

★ When considering why you are pursuing a legal career, think about what you would like to accomplish during law school and, in the future, as an attorney.

★ If you are passionate about a specific area of legal practice, include this in your message, but don't forget to explain why.

Use the questions below to think in more detail about your identity as a law student. Consider the sample student answers given. Are yours similar? How do they differ?

WHO ARE YOU?

What drives you?

"I am driven by my desire to help others."

What life experiences stand out to you?

"In high school, I had the opportunity to volunteer for a legal clinic that specialized in disability rights for minors. While my responsibilities were mostly relegated to faxing and photocopying, I was able to observe client conferences and watch how attorneys helped our clients get the support they needed."

Why are your life experiences important?

"This experience challenged my views of equality and served as the impetus for my passion to study public interest law."

WHY ARE YOU HERE?

Why did you go to law school?

"After taking the time to consider what I would like to do after university, I decided that practicing law would give me the power to try to make a difference in my community through legislation."

Why is studying law important to you?

"Studying law is important to me because the knowledge I will gain will prove useful not only for my own life, but also the lives of others."

What do you hope to achieve with your degree?

"I came to law school to better understand the law and how it applies to legislation on all levels. I intend to apply what I have learned as an elected official in my community."

In two to three sentences, explain why you are pursuing a legal career.

"I have a true passion for advocating for others. Pursuing a legal career will allow me not only to advocate for others, but also to teach them how to advocate for themselves."

CELEBRATE YOUR INDIVIDUALITY

Does or should your culture, ethnicity, sexuality, personality, or individuality play a role in how you are perceived academically and professionally? The short answer to this question is "yes." All of your experiences have informed who you are today. These experiences, whether positive or negative, influence your actions, reactions, and decisions.

THE ROLE OF DIVERSITY

In the context of the workplace, diversity is desirable. And diversity extends beyond just race, to cover gender, sexuality, economic status, educational background, language, age, religion, and more. First, we encouraged you to reflect upon your life and career goals. Now you should consider the characteristics that make you unique.

Equally important, your employer should appreciate how your perspective can add depth and value. If being accepted and included for who you are is woven into your success, consider researching an employer's commitment to diversity.

Pro tips

CELEBRATE YOU!

★ As you formulate your answers to the questions opposite, remember that you need only share the parts of you that you are comfortable sharing. You don't have to dissect your entire personality, simply highlight the elements that make you stand out among your peers.

★ If there is a characteristic for which you are unapologetic and that you feel you must express, do it. It is important that you present your true self, honestly, in order for you to determine whether you are the correct "fit" for a future employer.

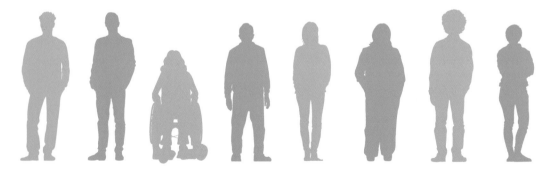

For example, does the employer actively seek diverse employees? What are the employee demographics? Does the employer actively participate in mentoring relationships for first-generation students? Are there partners of diverse backgrounds? It's a good sign when an employer already has an established diversity and inclusion commitment. See also Chapter Sixteen: Diversity, Inclusion, and Equity.

Use the questions below to think about the traits that make you who you are. Consider the sample student answers given and how they compare to yours.

WHAT MAKES YOU, YOU?

Which elements of your identity do you value most?

"My family played an important role in who I have become. They have always accepted me as I am and encouraged me to be true to myself."

What are your strengths?

"I have a keen ability to spot and mediate issues. This strength has proven useful personally and professionally."

What is your proudest achievement?

"To date, I am most proud of returning to and finishing university. I was side-tracked by a few life experiences along the way, but I am proud that I worked toward achieving a life-long goal."

What is your biggest failure?

"I will never forget my biggest failure. I was working for a bank and just restocked the cash drawer with crisp new money. At the end of the day, my drawer was over two hundred dollars short. This hard lesson taught me to check and double-check my work and to pay attention—especially when handling money!"

In two to three sentences, what makes you different from your peers?

"Growing up, our family had a motto: 'We Never Give Up.' I have found that even in the most challenging situation, I have been able to rise to the occasion and meet or exceed expectations."

PRESENTING YOURSELF
PROFESSIONALLY

Most law schools do not require you to wear a suit to class. For other events, however, you should always think about appropriate attire, with consideration to the venue and type of event.

FIRST IMPRESSIONS

Once you have committed to attending the law school of your choice, and before you begin your first class, you will most likely be invited to various events, such as open houses, admitted student days, and a new student orientation. How you present yourself at these events is important, as this will be an opportunity to create an excellent first impression to your colleagues, professors, law school administration, and possibly future employers.

"What you wear is how you present yourself to the world, especially today, when human contacts are so quick."

Miuccia Prada, fashion designer

DAY-TO-DAY

You must wear a suit to an interview, but what do you wear for a meeting with your professor, an informational interview with an alumnus of the school, or an evening bar association event? You may be thinking that what you wear is not nearly as important as what you say and how you behave. In most settings, this would be true. But you have chosen to become a member of one of the most conservative professions there is. As such, you are still required to wear a suit to court, in meetings with clients, and to the office, so prepare yourself.

DRESSING PROFESSIONALLY

1 The right suit

You should have at least two matching suits (one plain navy suit and one plain black suit) in your possession upon entering law school. Note that two items of the same color does not a full suit make! Due to the many styles and textures available, it is difficult to match different jackets and bottoms. Pairing your pants or skirt with a sport coat or blazer does not constitute a full suit and is considered unacceptable dress for an interview. While skirt suits are considered most conservative for women, in the last decade, pant suits have become increasingly acceptable.

2 Suits for hire

If you find that you are unable to afford a suit, talk to your career services or student affairs offices. Some law schools have donated suits available for students.

3 Casualwear

Some employers may allow "casual Friday" dress, where you will have permission to wear jeans. In this case, dark jeans are acceptable, paired with a polo shirt, dress shirt, or blouse, and closed-toe shoes.

4 Plan ahead

When choosing your ensemble, always consider your schedule for the day. While you may be allowed to wear jeans to the office, you could be called into a meeting with your supervising attorney and a client or instructed to appear in court as a certified law student. Keep a blazer or sport coat in your car or office to avoid missed opportunities.

PROFESSIONAL ATTIRE OR BUSINESS FORMAL

Full matching suit and tie (optional for women); solid color

Skirt that is knee-length or below for women

Long-sleeve, button-down shirt

Top and bottoms purchased together in the same section of the store (if you purchased it online, the top and bottom should have matching garment names).

Dress/closed-toe shoes

Dress socks that match your shoes

BUSINESS ATTIRE OR BUSINESS CASUAL

When choosing your ensemble, always consider your schedule for the day.

Typically a sport coat or blazer with trousers or pants for men

Dress shirt, blouse, or polo shirt for women

Optional tie

Pants or dress/skirt that is knee-length or below

Dress shoes that cover all or most of the foot, or loafers

Bottoms do not have to match your coat

Cotton twill material is acceptable

BEHAVING PROFESSIONALLY

Gaining licensure to practice law is an arduous process. Not only must you graduate from law school or university, you must pass a rigorous background check (among other stringent requirements) that may require the auditing of your law school and undergraduate files, and/or participation in a training program. Exhibiting inappropriate behavior at law school could result in negative marks in your school file, so it is wise to behave professionally at all times.

THINK ABOUT YOUR ACTIONS

Treat others with the respect you expect them to show you. When you sit in class, a willing participant of the Socratic method, understand that the person sitting next to you may eventually sit across from you in a mediation or the courtroom. A classmate may turn out to be the person who will recommend you for a position to their employer. The person you cut off while driving to class could be your professor or future boss. The world is smaller than you think.

RECOGNIZE SUPPORT RESOURCES

Law school is filled with many different personalities, ideas, and opinions. However, if you find that the actions of colleagues negatively impact your ability to succeed, you have support systems to help you. Contact your law school's career advisor or a member of the student affairs department. Both are wonderful resources put in place to help you navigate law school and positively develop your career goals while providing a safe space to speak out about your frustrations.

CLEAN UP YOUR DIGITAL ACT

The Internet has a long memory, and anything that appears in a search engine's results page may be considered public knowledge. Employers routinely conduct Internet searches of prospective (and sometimes current) employees. If you haven't done so before now, open a search engine and search for yourself to examine your digital footprint. From now on, think about the ramifications of what you post on social media. More than a few have suffered for the type of information they have shared online. Free speech is not free of consequences.

Check your integrity

The unauthorized practice of law is a punishable offense and carries serious penalties. As a law student, you may not misrepresent yourself as a lawyer in any manner. You may not provide legal advice under the guise of a lawyer or someone experienced in the practice of law. If you are found guilty of this offense, there is little chance you will be permitted to practice law.

LIFELONG PROFESSIONALISM
Individuals who have successfully honed their craft understand the importance of lifelong personal and professional development. The information provided in this book should serve only as a starting point. It is up to you to remain focused on your goals and utilize all resources and opportunities to grow and succeed within your chosen profession.

Pro tips

LIFELONG PROFESSIONAL DEVELOPMENT IS KEY

★ If you become interested in a specific area of law, seek to master it. Join professional associations related to that practice area or research and write articles to familiarize yourself with the subject.

★ Be Innovative. Be Creative. Stay abreast of the ways technology and innovation contribute to the legal field. Are there new programs that help calculate billable hours more efficiently? Can Zoom meetings replace in-person meetings when distance presents an issue? Your ability to adapt to the changing landscape can ensure longevity and long-term success.

CHAPTER TEN

NETWORKING

As the saying goes, "It's not what you know, but who you know." Are you aware that the number-one way that law school graduates get their first legal position is through networking? Strategically developing your professional network will help you stand out from the crowd when you're looking for a job and may even give you an advantage when it comes to hearing about jobs in the first place. And networking doesn't have to involve awkward cocktail parties; there are ways to align it with your strengths and personality.

Networking is crucial to any job search experience, and you don't have to fear the experience. Introverts may choose to skip networking entirely to avoid finding themselves in uncomfortable situations. Inserting oneself into an unfamiliar situation is frightening for most people. But there is hope. Here's a secret: introverts and extroverts alike must prepare for the law school networking experience in the same way. If you haven't noticed by now, preparation is crucial and, if you answered the professional identity questions in the previous chapter, you're already halfway there!

To network efficiently and adequately, there are a few factors to consider. For example, you may ask yourself, "What is the purpose of the event you are attending?," and "What do you hope to gain from this experience?" Additionally, you are encouraged to utilize all networking platforms available to you. That's right—you can use social media to your advantage in creating your network of contacts. From LinkedIn to Instagram, you can create a personal brand that highlights your skills, abilities, and passion without ever leaving your home. In addition to honing your professional social presence, this chapter will discuss practical ways to connect with others in the legal field.

THE ELEVATOR PITCH

The urban legend of the "elevator pitch" began in old Hollywood when, supposedly, a screenwriter would "accidentally" catch an unsuspecting executive on an elevator ride, where they would be trapped for the time it took to move between floors. Usually, the screenwriter would have between 30 and 60 seconds to pitch their idea, in the hope of securing financing for their project. The elevator pitch has since evolved and today is used in all manner of professions to generate interest in a person, idea, or product.

YOUR PITCH

In law school, your elevator pitch should be clear and concise and express a brief and memorable message. In the last chapter, you practiced answering the questions "Who are you?" and "Why are you here?" Well this is your moment to shine: Using the information you have gathered about yourself, hone your pitch.

Pro tips

Your pitch should be:

★ 20 to 30 seconds in length

★ A positive representation of you

★ A brief explanation of why you are attending the event

★ Informative, including professional details such as your school year and your short- or long-term goals

Sample pitch

"Good evening. My name is Jane Doe and it's a pleasure to meet you. I'm a first-year law student at General School of Law, and I am excited to participate in this event. While my passion is working in public interest, it is my dream to start my own firm someday, and I would like to learn more about solo practitioners and how they got their start."

This is simple enough. You will notice that Jane hasn't shared much personal information but she has managed to express her passion, goals, and academic details. Try practicing your elevator pitch on family and friends, or with an advisor in your careers department. The more you practice, the less contrived and more sincere your pitch will sound.

BUSINESS CARDS

When an opportunity presents itself, having a business card can secure you an interview and, subsequently, a job. You may be able to obtain business cards from your school or you may have to create and print them yourself. Either way, it is important for you to have business cards and carry them with you always.

WHAT TO INCLUDE (AND NOT)

1. Adhere to your school's policies and guidelines when ordering business cards. You must receive permission to print a school logo for personal use.

2. Important information
- Your first and last name (you may include an appropriate nickname as well)
- Your school name
- Your year in school
- Your email address
- Your phone number
- Cocurricular activities, such as student organizations, or journal memberships

3. Do not place your picture or any other personal details on your business card.

YOUR CONTACTS

After any event you attend, gather any business cards you have collected and write a few details on the back of each to help you remember to whom you spoke and the content of the conversation. For example, if your contact was planning to vacation in your favorite place, write that information on the back. When you send a follow-up or thank you email, you can reference their upcoming vacation and perhaps suggest a few places they might visit. Doing this firmly sets you apart from others and your contact may remember you based on your conversation.

Sample business cards

Jane Doe
General School of Law

- Juris Doctor Candidate, May 2023
- Member, Public Interest Law Foundation

(777) 777-7777
J.Doe@LawSchool.edu

James "Jimmy" Doe
General School of Law

- Juris Doctor Candidate, May 2023
- Moot Court Member
- Student Representative, Student Bar Association

(777) 777-7777
J.Doe@LawSchool.edu

INFORMATIONAL INTERVIEWS

Informational interviews are a great way to obtain more information about a person without the pressure of interviewing for a position. The informational interview places you in the driver's seat. You are responsible for asking questions to learn more about the person and their area of practice. It is important to note that informational interviews can sometimes morph into real interviews; you may even find yourself with a job offer—a great reason to take any informational interview seriously and plan properly.

SECURING AN INFORMATIONAL INTERVIEW

Reaching out to a stranger to inquire about their life and gain information about the legal field can seem more than a little off-putting. However, in addition to making connections at professional events, there are other ways to speak with legal professionals. Approach your law school's careers office to find out about alumni practicing in your preferred practice area. This is the easiest place to start because they are in regular contact with alumni. You can also draw on LinkedIn and other professional websites to create a list of potential contacts.

PREPARING FOR THE INFORMATIONAL INTERVIEW

★ Research the attorney
★ Bring business cards
★ Bring a resume (but only provide it on request)
★ Prepare an agenda of what you would like to discuss and include five to ten questions to ask the interviewer (see below)
★ Wear a suit to the meeting

After the interview, remember to send a thank you email or note (see opposite).

Sample questions to ask during an informational interview

? What do you like most/least about your job?

? What does a typical day look like for you?

? Tell me about your practice.

? How do you balance the demands of a legal career with family obligations?

Sample informational interview request

Sample follow-up thank-you letter

 **NEW MESSAGE**

SUBJECT: Thank you

Dear Ms. Banks,

Thank you for taking the time to speak with me at yesterday's bar association event for solo practitioners. It was a pleasure meeting you. I especially enjoyed talking about your upcoming vacation to Maui. As you may recall, Maui is one of my favorite places. I highly suggest visiting Black Rock and swimming with the wild sea turtles. While the area is a little touristy, the waters are clear and beautiful.

I also enjoyed speaking with you about how you started your firm and will take to heart the tips you provided on how to approach my real estate law class. I am particularly interested in landlord/tenant law and I know that you have centered your practice around these issues. Should your schedule allow, I would like to continue our conversation to further discuss this practice area in person or over the phone.

Thank you again, and I look forward to hearing from you.

Sincerely,

Jimmy Doe
General School of Law
Class of 2023
(777) 777-7777

✉ **NEW MESSAGE**

SUBJECT: Informational Interview

Dear Ms. Banks,

My name is Jane Doe and I am a student at General School of Law. I received your contact information via my law school's alumni department and am honored to make your acquaintance.

I am contacting you because of your wealth of experience in real estate law. Specifically, I am interested in landlord/tenant law, and I know that you have centered your practice around these issues. I understand that managing your own firm ensures that you are constantly busy, and I place tremendous value on your time. As such, I am requesting just 20–30 minutes to speak with you for a brief informational interview next week. I look forward to hearing from you.

Sincerely,

Jane Doe
General School of Law
Class of 2023
(777) 777-7777

? What have you learned while practicing law that you wish you had known while in law school?

? What can I do during law school to prepare for work in the legal field?

? What are some practical skills that you feel all attorneys should have upon graduation?

ALTERNATIVE WAYS TO NETWORK

In any profession, becoming a master at your craft requires passion, motivation, and creativity. The same is true for your career as a burgeoning attorney. Speak to attorneys in various settings to gain a global perspective on how to approach your career path. Consider the following when sketching your career plan.

TALK TO YOUR PROFESSORS

Law professors come to the profession with a wealth of experience in specific practice areas. In their past life, professors may have practiced law as solo practitioners, judges, attorneys at large firms, public interest organization directors, and so on. They represent a largely untapped resource. As you register for your legal courses, research the professors' backgrounds and work experience. By reviewing their biography on the school's website, you will learn a lot about a professor's passions and what drives them to do the work they do. If you find that you are doing well in a specific class, contact that professor and ask if they need a faculty research assistant.

JOIN A PROFESSIONAL LEGAL ASSOCIATION

There are many different types of legal associations and they may allow student members. These associations vary based on region, gender, ethnicity, practice area, you name it. There are legal professional associations for many common interests. Joining a legal association is especially helpful for law students because they provide training, programming, online content, and networking events that are vital to honing your professional development. Start with organizations that are in your region. This will make it easier for you to attend events and make connections.

BAR ASSOCIATIONS

★ After joining a legal association, volunteer at events or help with programming. This is a great way to meet and work with practicing attorneys and increase your network of contacts. When one of their colleagues is in need of a law clerk, who do you think they will suggest? That's right, you!

★ Remember to research the legal association prior to joining. Knowing the organization's mission and values will lead to better conversations and will inevitably answer the question, "Why are you here?"

BECOME A RESEARCH ASSISTANT

Welcome to the inner sanctum. Jokes aside, faculty research assistant (RA) positions are prestigious and help you gain practical legal experience while earning school credit or income. Because faculty members are consistently publishing their work in books, articles, and professional writings, working as an RA will provide you with the opportunity to research hot-button or cutting-edge issues relevant to the legal field. Additionally, you will learn proper research techniques that will serve you throughout your legal career. Working for a law professor can also increase your network of contacts exponentially, as they may also introduce you to their peers. If you do well and have formed a great professional relationship, the professor may provide a recommendation for other prestigious positions, such as judicial clerkships. Remember, becoming an RA is as simple as asking. If you have an interest in a specific practice area, you can suggest a project to your professor. If the professor does not need help with research, ask if they have colleagues who need RAs.

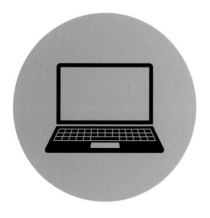

"The chance to work with a law professor as a research assistant is a golden opportunity. The student receives one-on-one guidance in the development of their research skills."

Ronnie R. Gipson Jr., visiting Assistant Professor of Law, Cecil C. Humphreys School of Law

ONLINE PROFESSIONAL NETWORKING

In the last few years, membership of online professional networking sites has increased exponentially. Professionals have found a new and innovative way to meet others in their field and fields that they would like to know more about. Sites such as LinkedIn provide a vast network of resources, contacts, and even available positions. Additionally, members have formed groups based on interests, practice areas, and so on.

Becoming a member of a professional networking site is the gift that keeps on giving. You can create a profile right now and begin meeting people in the legal field. You don't have to wait to start law school to begin this stage of networking. As with all other types of professional networking, though, you must take it seriously.

CONNECTING WITH OTHERS

You can use online professional networking sites to connect with other professionals in your field. Take 15 minutes out of your day each week to research profiles of individuals with whom you would like to connect. Send personalized messages through the site to briefly explain why you are reaching out. In addition to reaching out to those you don't know, connect with professionals with whom you have worked and ask them to recommend or endorse any skills and abilities they believe you possess. Consider returning the favor and serve as an endorser for them too.

STAY IN THE KNOW

Apprising yourself of industry trends within the legal field is a great way to stay connected to those you've met or who you'd like to meet. If you find a particularly interesting article, send it to a contact. Consider responding to articles that are of particular interest to you. Of course, you must remain professional—and mind your grammar—but doing this demonstrates interest while learning more about a specific area.

CREATING YOUR PROFILE

Your profile should consist of all of your past work experience, volunteer activities, interests, and awards and it is not simply a reiteration of your resume. First-year law school students are encouraged to apply to positions using resumes that are only one page in length. An online profile will allow you to expound upon your experience and present a 3D version of yourself. Feel free to go into detail about all you have accomplished in all of your positions. Did you exceed sales goals? How about that policy handbook you drafted that increased productivity by 35%? Place this information on your profile as well. Take advantage of this opportunity to sell your professional self.

Name (or Nickname):

Jane Doe

Summary:

Legal studies student with demonstrated interest in family law, immigration law, and landlord/tenant law. I possess practical legal experience in drafting legal documents and performing legal research.

Education:

General University College of Law, Los Angeles, CA
Juris Doctor Candidate, May 2021

John C. Brooks University, Detroit, MI
Bachelor of Science, Mathematics, May 2018

Work experience:

Banks and Banks, Los Angeles, CA
Law Clerk, May 2020—September 2020

- Researched legal materials and case law pertaining to family and immigration laws and drafted memoranda for submission to supervising attorney
- Observed trials and debriefed with attorneys
- Conducted intake interviews for pro bono clients

For the People Organization, Los Angeles, CA
Fellow, May 2019—September 2019

- Researched cases regarding housing and landlord/tenant laws
- Communicated with clients regarding case information such as court dates and attorney meetings

Volunteer experience:

General University, Public Interest Legal Foundation, President, 2018–2020

York Community Center, Volunteer Tutor, 2017–2020

Nora E. Cloud Elementary, Mathlete Coach, 2016–2017

Specialized skills or languages:

Certified, Lexis/Westlaw Researcher

Fluent, Spanish; fluent, Italian

Professional memberships:

Member, Lemon County Bar Association

Student Outreach Chair, Immigration Attorney section of the Lemon County Bar Association

Member, Speech Masters International

VIRTUAL NETWORKING

During the worldwide COVID-19 pandemic, professionals from every area, including the law, had to pivot to virtual conferencing to adjust to social guidelines. Professionals in the legal field took advantage of the ability to meet with each other using virtual collaboration platforms and this form of communication has since become the norm.

IN THE CLASSROOM

The rapid shift from in-person to distance learning forced students and professors to make extreme adjustments. Before the pandemic, a student would simply have made an appointment with their professor and met them in their office to discuss previous lectures or assignments. Now, students must try to create an academic relationship through a computer screen. So how does this dynamic change relationships? The lofty answer would be that it shouldn't change anything. However, this is not the case as "Zoom Fatigue" and "Zoom Gloom" are very real. While constant virtual conferencing can be taxing, as a future lawyer, you must remain professional and consider that your brand is attached to your actions regardless of your location. Therefore, set yourself up for distance learning success by creating an academic schedule, a personal schedule, staying in contact with your professors, and school staff, and your friends and family.

NETWORKING AND INTERVIEWING

There is a silver lining to the rapid shift to virtual conferencing. Now, you can converse with professionals in the legal field all over the globe. This isn't to say that the technology didn't exist before. However, professionals in the legal field are more accepting of this style of communication. So, take advantage of this opportunity to make as many professional legal connections as you are able! Securing a virtual informational or real interview or even participating in a Zoom networking event is now a much easier task to accomplish.

CAREER FAIRS

Universities have already held countless virtual career fairs and they offer all of the same opportunities as in-person events. Some even set aside time where students can network with legal professionals.

Pro tips

VIRTUAL MEETINGS

★ When scheduling a virtual meeting, make sure you are in a quiet area and that your Internet connection and browser support the platform you are using.

★ Approach your virtual meetings the same way that you would an in-person meeting. Wear a full suit and prepare an agenda.

Wearing a suit to a virtual meeting is an expression of your sincerity; preparing an agenda ensures your time is spent productively.

CHAPTER ELEVEN

INTERVIEWING

Keeping your momentum going requires practice and patience—it's a marathon, not a sprint. You need to be clear on your goals, with a deep understanding of what you're looking for and what you have to offer. But like a marathon, you can do it with structured training and advice from folks who have been there.

The ability to interview well is essential in any profession, especially in law, since it relies heavily on communication skills. An interview is your first test in your ability to communicate and advocate for yourself. You will be asked questions like "Why should we hire you?" or "How do you think you can positively contribute to our team?" Identifying your abilities to provide evidence as to why you should be hired is key and requires preparation beforehand. Legal interviews can also be unpredictable, taking a half-day or more as you meet with different people. Interview styles and techniques may vary and are sometimes employed simultaneously. Understanding the process and knowing when and how to answer tough interview questions will set you apart from your colleagues.

As you progress in your legal studies, the expectations of legal employers increases exponentially. For example, by your first round of interviews in your first year, employers do not expect polished responses and a resume peppered with practical legal skills. However, by your second year, the expectation is for you to navigate the process with confidence while dutifully explaining the legal skills you have gained with precision. This chapter will discuss application materials such as cover letters and resumes, as well as interviewing styles and techniques to properly prepare you for interviewing during law school.

EMPLOYMENT OPPORTUNITIES

As you progress through your legal studies, your employment opportunities will increase. The key to a successful academic career is not just about achieving high marks. It is important to gain, and subsequently hone, your research and writing skills, and other expertise such as litigation and negotiation through practical legal experience. Each year, you should expound upon the knowledge you've gained as you take steps closer to becoming an excellent lawyer.

FIRST YEAR

Your first interview for a legal position may occur early in your spring term where you will have the opportunity to meet with employers seeking law clerks or externs for the summer before your second year. You may be eligible to participate in a spring job fair or on-campus interviews for positions with government agencies, public interest organizations, corporations, and law firms. You should receive ample notification of spring semester opportunities from your careers office, student organization representative, or faculty members.

MIDDLE YEARS

In the summer after your first year of law school, you may have the opportunity to interview for large firms through their on-campus interview programs. These jobs are especially competitive, as you are likely to be vying for positions with students from other top-ranked law schools. Interviews may take place the summer before your second year and will commence in May or June in the summer before your third year. Essentially, you will be interviewing almost one year in advance for a summer position and almost two years in advance for a post-graduate position.

Why are these positions so competitive? The short answer is the large applicant pool, coupled with a limited amount of positions at each firm, and post-graduate salaries of upwards of $145,000 per year. The highest reported salary of new associates at a few of these firms is around $190,000 (National Association for Law Placement, 2019).

National and international firms generally recruit from tier-one law schools. If you attend a tier-two law school or below, and

Pro tips

STAY ON TOP OF EMAILS

Always check your school email, as this is the primary method of communication of cocurricular departments such as Career Services and Student Affairs. Neglecting to check your email is the easiest way to miss out on great interview and job opportunities.

would like to interview with a large firm, you will need to make yourself as competitive as possible. Important factors in your ability to compete are grades, participation in a school journal where research and writing are tantamount, such as law review, membership on a moot court or mock trial team, practical legal experience, and of course, stellar application materials. See also Chapter Five: Legal Research and Writing Beyond Law School.

Be competitive

 Grade point average (GPA): Take your first year seriously. Interviewing for prestigious firms or government agencies largely depends on your GPA and class rank.

 Research and writing: Law review and other peer-reviewed scholastic journals are a great way to gain research and writing experience.

 Courtroom experience: Mock trial/moot court (competition and casebook) provide practical legal experience equivalent to a courtroom that is invaluable to law clerks.

 Practical experience: The expectation for all students is to seek practical legal experience. The ability to converse with a potential employer about your practical legal experience may set you apart from your peers. See also Chapter Twelve: Internships and Externships and Chapter 13: Judicial Clerkships.

 Application materials: Your application materials must be perfect. Meticulously review your resume, cover letter, and writing sample prior to submission. It is firmly suggested that you meet with a careers advisor to discuss your materials.

APPLICATION DOCUMENTS

The documents you submit to any employer represent your first writing sample. Therefore, it is imperative that these materials contain zero errors. By the spring term of your first year (or as early as the end of your first term), you will be asked to submit, at the very minimum, a resume, cover letter, and a writing sample. Drafting these materials beforehand will help ensure that you do not miss out on job opportunities. It's also a good idea to consult your careers office for sample application materials prior to drafting your own—don't neglect this valuable resource!

LEGAL RESUME

The formatting of a legal resume is very different from a nonlegal resume. For example, legal resumes are much more concise and contain relevant legal experience, if available. If this is your first professional career, your resume should be one page in length. Public interest legal resumes may be more than one page if you have relevant public service experience. An employer should be able to read your entire resume in 20 to 30 seconds.

Remember, your resume is not a complete autobiography—it is only a snapshot of your experience.

Whether you have recently graduated or have been away from school for many years, the education section of your resume is the first section of the document. This signals to the reviewer that you are currently in school. Always double-check your contact information.

Pro tips

STAY PREPARED

In your legal position, always keep a log of all of your tasks, responsibilities, and accomplishments. Having this information readily available will make it easier for you to draft your resume.

JANE DOE
Address; City, State/Country; (888) 888-8888
Professional email address; LinkedIn URL

EDUCATION

Generic Law School, City, State
Juris Doctor Candidate, May 2023
Member, Public Interest Law Society

Generic University, City, State
Bachelor of Science, Biology, June 2020
Member, Premed Honors Society, 2018–2020
Member, Associated Student Union, 2017–2020

RELEVANT EXPERIENCE

Doe, Doe & Doe, City, State
Law Clerk, May 2020–Present
Research and draft legal brief on specific issues relating to immigration law
for submission to supervising attorney.
*(Begin all sentences with a present action verb if you are currently working,
and past tense if you are no longer employed in the position. Be clear and
concise and provide evidence. For example, if you conducted legal research,
explain what you did with the information you gathered and to who(m)
this information was submitted.)*

Coffee Express, City, State
Barista, May 2018–May 2020
Prepared and served made-to-order specialty coffee drinks and teas.
Managed inventory of coffee beans, brewing equipment, and bathroom supplies.

COMMUNITY ACTIVITIES

Volunteer, Homeless Youth of America, 2015–Present
Canvasser, Mickey M. for Senate District 28, 2019

LANGUAGE SKILLS

Fluent Spanish: Reading, writing, and translation

COVER LETTERS

A cover letter is a persuasive document. The goal of a cover letter is to encourage the reviewer to invite you to an interview. Your cover letter should be specific to the employer and position. Generic cover letters are a waste of time because they are insincere and usually end up in the trash. Do not waste your time, and the employer's time, by submitting a generic cover letter.

Your cover letter should be a combination of hard and soft skills. Regardless of your experience, your cover letter should be one page (usually four to five paragraphs in total). Be clear and concise and keep things relevant to the position to which you are applying. Format your cover letter properly. The letterhead on your cover letter needs to match your resume.

Pro tips

PROCEED WITH CONFIDENCE

Don't be intimidated by writing a cover letter. This is the perfect opportunity to showcase your excellent and persuasive writing skills! When emailing an application, be sure to send any required documents as PDF attachments.

Structuring a cover letter

★ The introductory paragraph should contain your year in school, law school name, the position and name of the firm to which you are applying, and why you are interested in the position as well as the practice area.

★ Supporting paragraphs, no more than two, should discuss your relevant experience as it relates to the position and speak to why an employer should hire you. If you are working, or have worked in a legal setting, briefly explain your tasks and responsibilities and provide examples. Statements that are not backed by examples are considered "throwaway statements" and make for a poor cover letter.

★ In addition to discussing your hard skills (research, writing, and so on), you should also write about your soft skills. Hard skills show that you can do the job, while soft skills show whether an employer can work with you.

★ In the final paragraph, reiterate your interest in the position.

YOUR ADDRESS
DATE

RECIPIENT'S ADDRESS

Dear (name of recipient),

I am a first-year law student at General Law School, and I write to apply for the open law clerk position with Banks, Banks & Banks for next summer. I am particularly interested in this position because of your firm's excellent reputation in immigration and family law. As evidenced by my experience, I have a strong commitment to these practice areas.

    As a sociology major at State University, I secured a legal intern position for JusticeNow!, a prestigious public service organization that focused on immigration and asylum cases. Over the course of three years, I honed my writing, research, and communication skills. For example, I was tasked with researching local and national immigration laws and drafting memoranda on my findings for submission to my supervisor. My responsibilities also included coordinating pop-up legal clinics where I and other volunteers assisted over 300 clients with completing immigrations forms. Working in this position also helped me hone my Spanish translation skills as I was frequently called upon to translate for clients during intake interviews, client meetings, and depositions. This position not only confirmed my interest in pursuing the law, it awakened my passion for immigration law.

    Prior to working for JusticeNow!, I volunteered for the family law clinic that was run by General University. This clinic provided free legal services to underserved communities and victims of domestic violence. This experience was especially rewarding as I was able to assist clients while learning about the law. For example, I conducted intake interviews, answered and fielded phone calls through a 24-hour hotline, and coordinated community awareness events. This entire experience was the impetus to my interest in the law.

    I am very interested in working for your firm and hope to have the opportunity to apply my experience and enthusiasm to this position. I look forward to meeting with you to further discuss my skills and experience.

Sincerely,

Jane Doe
Juris Doctor Candidate

Attachment(s): Resume, Writing Sample, and Transcripts

SUPPORTING MATERIALS

Employers often request additional materials to accompany a resume and cover letter. These materials present a more well-rounded applicant and can provide the basis for a more in-depth interview.

WRITING SAMPLE

Be prepared to submit a writing sample to an employer in the second semester of your first year—you may use an assignment from your legal writing class. Use one you wrote while on the job. Ask your supervising attorney for permission to use a document you have written since, for example, confidential information may need to be redacted. Note writing sample requirements on job descriptions, as they may detail guidelines such as writing sample length.

TRANSCRIPT OF GRADES

Applications are generally submitted online. Therefore, keep an updated, digital copy of your academic transcript. Only submit an official academic transcript if requested. Contact your student records department for information on how to order an official academic transcript. Additionally, note your class rank. Some schools provide a class rank on your academic transcript.

REFERENCE LIST

The hardest part of drafting a reference list is deciding which of your references to place on it. Your list of references should be a combination of employers and professors, but should include no more than three references in total. You can have different versions of your list depending on where you are applying. For example, you may have been a research assistant for a professor who teaches an intellectual property course, as well as a few legal references in the same field. Save this as your "IP Reference List."

PERSONAL STATEMENT

Diversity positions in law firms, with public interest firms, or government agencies may require a personal statement, or even a brief viewpoint on a specific topic. A personal statement is not a cover letter and unless otherwise instructed, may be longer than one page. In writing your personal statement, read and take notes on the prompt before you begin your draft. For example, an employer may ask you to explain, in no more than eight paragraphs, why you are interested in public interest law and how you have demonstrated your interest in this area throughout your life.

Pro tips

BE SELECTIVE

Only submit documents that are requested by the employer. Reviewing applications is an arduous process and additional documents may not be read.

"References are helpful; they speak to your interest in a specific practice area."

INTERVIEW PREPARATION

Now that you have secured an interview, it's time to do a bit of research. Taking the time to prepare yourself properly will set you apart from your peers and will set you up for success. Review the information below to prepare yourself for your next big step!

EMPLOYER

When researching an employer start with their website. Whatever you see on the first page is what they want you to know. If there is a picture of boxing gloves or lawyers meeting with people in the community, they want the visitor to understand that they will fight for you!

Consider researching the firm through Lexis Nexis or Westlaw. Review cases they have won and note interesting details that you can talk about during an interview. This is a great way to stand out in an interview.

INTERVIEWER

Confirm the name of your interviewer(s) and research them on LinkedIn and other professional networking sites. If you know your interviewer is an alumnus of the school, talk to your alumni department to find out more.

POSITION

Save the job listing for every position to which you apply. Having the job listing on hand when preparing for an interview is very helpful. Read the job listing and formulate questions you would like to ask during the interview.

Pro tips

DRESS APPROPRIATELY

As mentioned in the previous chapter, dressing professionally, particularly for an interview, demonstrates two important facts about you right away:

1) That you are serious about the position.

2) That you care about your personal brand. Wearing a full suit to an interview is expected. All shoes must be closed toe and may be brown, black, or navy.

Questions to ask

From the research you gathered for the interview, prepare questions to ask the interviewer. Sample questions may include:

★ What are your expectations for this position?

★ Can you tell me about the most successful person you've ever hired/worked with and what they did to be successful?

★ How would you describe the work environment here?

★ Who will supervise my work?

DO NOT ask the following questions:

★ How many hours am I required to work?

★ What is the pay for this position? (If not posted, wait for the offer to inquire about pay and possible negotiation.)

PRACTICE AREA

One of the biggest mistakes students make during legal interviews is failing to discover which area of law is practiced by the employer. Double-check the office to which you are applying and confirm the practice areas in that office.

KNOW YOURSELF

Know your resume from top to bottom. On a sheet of paper, review the positions you listed on your resume and write the hard and soft skills you gained. If applicable, review the "interests" section of your resume. If you stated that you love baking and baseball, be prepared to answer questions on each.

MOCK INTERVIEW

Contact your career services or a mentor in the field of law in which you will be interviewing. Schedule a mock interview to hone your interview skills and receive constructive criticism on your interview ability. Prepare for your mock interview the same way you would a real interview. Wear a suit. It is important to make the atmosphere as real as possible so as to make the most of the experience.

BEHAVIORAL INTERVIEWING

There are various interview styles that are utilized to deduce competencies. Interviews can range from panel interviews, to behavioral, situational, or structured. Reviewing your resume and preparing yourself will help with most, but one specific style of interview requires a bit more planning. Behavioral interviewing is still widely used in interview settings.

TYPE OF QUESTION

Most behavioral interview questions are framed to cause further reflection while acquiring specific information for the employer. In the question posed in the scenario here, the employer would like to know how you deal with challenging situations. Are you able to think on your feet, and will you ask for help? Believe it or not, there is a correct way to answer this question. If you have heard of it, utilizing the S.T.A.R. method is the easiest and most precise way to answer these types of questions successfully.

"Tell me about a time when you were given a project and you had no idea how to proceed?"

Pro tips

TOP FIVE!

In preparing for your interview, think of five characteristics that you believe define who you are and make you different from other interviewees. Having this information at the forefront of your brain will help you successfully answer the "Why should we hire YOU?" question.

THE STAR METHOD

Situation
This is the setting to your story.
"While working in a law firm during
my second summer . . ."

Task
Explain the task that you were given.
" . . . I was tasked with drafting a motion
and I had no idea where to begin . . . "

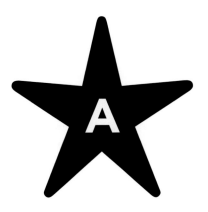

Action
Talk about the action you took to
complete the task.
" . . . So, I researched samples and spoke
with the office paralegal and asked for tips
on how to properly proceed . . . "

Result
Discuss whether you were
successful and reflect on what you learned.
"I submitted my motion to my supervising
attorney and they made just a few changes
and my sparsely edited motion was granted.
I learned a lot from this experience.
For example, I learned the importance of
working independently while also utilizing
the great resources in the office."

YOUR BIG INTERVIEW CHECKLIST

You've done it! You followed directions, submitted a perfect application, and prepared for your interview ad nauseum. All you need to do now is take a deep breath and take care of a few logistics.

THE DAY BEFORE THE INTERVIEW

 Confirm travel time, parking, and interview location.

 Check your gas levels if you are driving.

 Press suit and prepare wardrobe.

 Gather application materials and place several copies in a black leather folio.

 If your interview will be conducted through a video conferencing platform, be sure to 1) test your technology, 2) find a quiet place to interview and remove distracting items from your wall, 3) check your lighting, and 4) confirm your name on the platform (be sure it is professional).

THE BIG DAY

 Your interview begins the moment you leave your door. Give yourself enough time so that you are not speeding to your destination and driving disrespectfully.

 When you arrive, be respectful of everyone you meet, from the parking attendant to the front desk assistant. Legal assistants and paralegals are highly respected in their office and treating them disrespectfully can cost you your job.

 Review your "top five" to prepare yourself (see page 146).

Email thank-you letters to your interviewers (and the person who set up the interview if they are different) within 24 hours. This is important, as decisions may be made quickly. Some employers also appreciate a handwritten note thanking them for their time and briefly reiterating your interest in the position.

 Your thank-you letter should be no more than three paragraphs and should reiterate your interest in the position. If you had an especially memorable conversation, briefly refer to it in your letter. This will help you stand out from your peers.

 Your thank-you letter should be formatted the same as your cover letter if you are going to attach it in an email as a PDF. If your email will serve as the letter, remember to speak professionally and use proper salutations. "Dear Ms. Banks" is an acceptable salutation. If the interviewer or employer has not responded to you in two weeks, send a kindly worded email inquiring about the status of the position.

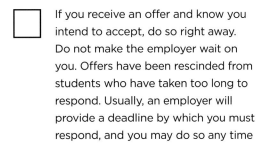 If you receive an offer and know you intend to accept, do so right away. Do not make the employer wait on you. Offers have been rescinded from students who have taken too long to respond. Usually, an employer will provide a deadline by which you must respond, and you may do so any time during that period.

 If you receive more than one offer, ask for an extension. If you have not heard from all employers but have received an offer, be prepared to accept the offer in hand.

 Do not apply to, or interview with, employers with whom you do not wish to work. This is simply unproductive and may strain your future professional relationship with the employer and your career services office.

CHAPTER TWELVE

INTERNSHIPS AND EXTERNSHIPS

Upon entering your legal studies, you are immediately held to the high standard set forth by the profession. So, as soon as you become a law student, you're a professional. That means you need to put your best foot forward from day one. After all, it's never too early to make a good impression.

You will have the opportunity to begin applying to legal positions as early as three months into your law school career. With that in mind, it is important to note which of your academic courses interest you and why. While you may attend law school to specialize in a specific practice area, you can develop interests in other areas as well. Participating in an internship or externship is beneficial because it can help you decide which area of law to pursue while helping you gain and hone your practical legal skills.

In addition to defining internships and externships, this chapter discusses the unwritten rules of professionalism, including what legal employers value and specific skills you should focus on developing. Because lawyers often specialize early in their careers, it's important to think long-term. You should choose an internship or externship carefully. Since it may lead to employment after law school, you'll want to make sure it's a good fit. Consider your future, your reasons for attending law school, and work toward making your dreams a reality!

EXTERNSHIPS VS. INTERNSHIPS

A legal externship is a paid or unpaid legal training program in a workplace, especially one offered to students as part of a course of study in return for school credit. A legal internship, or traineeship, is the position of a student or post-graduate trainee who works in an organization, usually for pay, in order to gain work experience in the legal field.

EXTERNSHIPS

In the United States, externships are usually formalized programs where students are supervised on-site by practicing attorneys for a duration of 8 to 14 weeks, depending on the semester. Because students receive credit for externships, employers must adhere to American Bar Association (ABA) standards on externships, which include oversight and feedback from supervising attorneys. Faculty members may also participate in additional oversight to confirm adherence to guidelines.

INTERNSHIPS

Legal internships offer an opportunity to gain practical legal experience in a variety of settings. Like externships, internships also provide many of the same benefits and opportunities for learning, with the possibility of a post-graduate position. While some employers may have formal internship programs, they are not subject to ABA standards for accreditation and may last an entire academic school year.

Benefits of externships

★ Practical legal experience on the job

★ Opportunity to build a professional network of contacts and lasting relationships

★ Exposure to a specific practice area

★ Potential to secure a post-graduate position

★ Resume building experience

★ Can do more than one in different practice areas to gain perspective and confirm preference

Both externships and internships can be of the following types:

Public interest; government agency; judicial; in a law firm; or with a company/corporation.

Internships may also be congressional.

"Participating in a legal externship is a wonderful way to gain practical experience that could lead to a post-graduate position."

YOUR JOB SEARCH

Locating and applying to legal positions is not as hard as you think. When you have decided your practice area preference, make an appointment to speak with your careers advisor. Don't reinvent the wheel. Your advisor serves as a gatekeeper, through their job-posting database, for many of the positions that come through the law school.

ON-CAMPUS INTERVIEWS

As mentioned in the previous chapters, the on-campus interview (OCI) is exactly what it sounds like. This is an interview that is held on-campus for legal positions that begin in the summer, spring, or fall. See also pages 136–137: Employment Opportunities.

LOCAL AND NATIONAL JOB FAIRS

Job fairs provide excellent opportunities in general and specialized practice areas. For example, you could participate in a public interest, intellectual property, or diversity job fair.

EXTERNSHIP OFFICES

Law schools in the United States usually have separate offices, specializing in externships, that house externship opportunities in prestigious positions. Are you interested in working for a judge (judicial extern), or externing for a major entertainment company? Check with your externship office.

ONLINE JOB SEARCHES

A simple Internet search will yield many results on specific positions. When searching online, remember to search various names of the same position. For example, when searching for a law clerk position, consider querying a search with different names. Law clerks are also called "summer legal clerks" or "legal interns."

Pro tips

GOOD PRACTICE

★ Search contact or firm information on official legal licensing websites to confirm that attorneys are active members with no disciplinary actions.

★ Save time and set up email job alerts. Have your potential opportunities come to you!

UNSPOKEN RULES OF PROFESSIONALISM

Perspective is key. When you begin any legal position, think about your personal goals and expectations. Write down all that you hope to accomplish as this is resume-worthy information you will use in your next interview.

You are not only in your position for a paycheck, you are also there to gain as much knowledge and practical experience as possible. Students who recognize this consistently receive offers. Employers offer orientations and networking lunches with the intention of immersing you in their office culture while expressly providing policy and regulations information. This is all done for a reason. Pay attention and do not passively participate in a position that you have waited your whole life to get. Instead, consider your surroundings, learn as much as you can, and use your skills to become a successful attorney. Not following the rules listed below could cost you your position and burn professional bridges in the future. Remember, you not only represent yourself, but your future self, your firm, and your law school.

On-the-job checklist

☑ Respect seniority

☑ Treat everyone with respect

☑ Respond to emails within 24 hours

☑ Communicate effectively and professionally

☑ If you worked as part of a team, share the credit

☑ Be on time

☑ Avoid gossip

☑ Be enthusiastic and show sincere interest

☑ Get out of your comfort zone and meet new people: network, network, network

☑ Minimize phone use during meetings

☑ Meet deadlines

☑ Use "reply all" sparingly

☑ Dress appropriately

☑ Observe and emulate proper professional behavior

YOUR FINAL YEAR OF LAW SCHOOL

By your final year of law school, you should have already gained legal experience. Hopefully, you will have secured a post-graduate position where you can immediately begin work as an attorney upon licensing. Ideally, you should spend your final year honing the relevant skills you have gained and seeking to gain a specialized understanding in your preferred practice area. Now is the time for you to add polish to your brand.

YOUR APPLICATION MATERIALS

Use the following as a guide for compiling a digital job search folder that keeps all of your application materials in one place. Check the materials frequently to see if any are in need of an update.

Writing samples

As stated previously, most employers request writing samples. In your third year, the expectation is for you to possess a writing sample written during a legal position (whether paid or unpaid). Remember to request permission from your employer or supervising attorney when deciding to use a document you drafted for work in deference to information that must remain confidential.

Resumes and cover letters

By now you will have written more than a few resumes and cover letters. Be sure to keep one resume that details all your work experience to date. Then create separate, pointed resumes for those positions that are specific to a practice area. Remember to label your resumes accordingly. The same is true for your cover letters. You should have several cover letters that address specific practice area interests to easily update allowing you to efficiently and quickly apply to job opportunities as they arise.

Pro tips

IT'S NEVER TOO LATE

If you have no legal experience and have not been successful in interviews, make an appointment to speak with your career advisor, mentor, or a contact in the field. You can still participate in on-campus interview programs and career fairs during the fall and spring terms of your last year of school. Utilize your resources and humbly consider their suggestions. You are only steps away from realizing your dream.

Networking and professional organizations

Hopefully, the ability to approach legal professionals and strike up a conversation should be old hat by your final year of school. The countless opportunities open to students in and out of school were available to you the moment you accepted your student status. Continue to attend events and take advantage of opportunities. Networking is a necessary skill as it not only provides the opportunity for job placement, but it will also get you clients.

Reference lists and recommendation letters

Seek to obtain at least three recommenders by your final year of law school. You may have a combination of professors and employers. If you have more than three, consider keeping a running list of recommenders and, much like your resumes and cover letters, keep separate lists determined by practice area. For example, you may have an immigration reference list (for applications to immigration law positions) that consists of an immigration professor, an immigration clinic supervising attorney, and a supervising attorney from an immigration law firm or government agency.

CHAPTER THIRTEEN

JUDICIAL CLERKSHIPS

Clerkships are an excellent opportunity to get a unique, behind-the-scenes view into the legal system and participate in deciding real cases and issues. Students are encouraged to do clerkships following law school since these positions provide an excellent experience that you can't get anywhere else.

Finding work as a judicial intern or post-graduate judicial clerk is prestigious owing to the inherent value of the role. The opportunity to sit with a judge and law clerks in chambers, to confer over opinions, observe courtroom etiquette, and hone your legal writing skills is invaluable— especially if you are seeking to practice criminal, civil, or appellate law. Further, judges and justices serve as wonderful mentors as well as recommenders for other positions. For those who are public-service minded, working for a judge may place you in the enviable position of providing input on various types of cases.

Suppose you find that you are academically competitive and have achieved high marks in courses focused on legal research and legal writing, working for a judge during law school or after may be a fulfilling career path for you. Because the application process is meticulous, this chapter describes judicial clerkship and judicial internship opportunities, applying to those positions, and the general expectations and responsibilities for a clerkship.

WHAT IS A JUDICIAL CLERKSHIP?

A clerkship offers an excellent opportunity to get a unique, behind-the-scenes view into the legal system and to participate in deciding real cases and issues. It provides an experience that you can't get anywhere else. Judicial clerkships bring invaluable access to judges where you have the opportunity to learn courtroom customs and procedures, and gain an accurate level of professionalism that is expected of lawyers.

JUDICIAL CLERK

A judicial clerk is a law school graduate who assists a judge in researching and deciding judicial matters. A traditional judicial clerkship is a paid position that takes place after law school and can last for one to two years. In the United States, a judicial clerk is not a judicial intern or judicial extern (generally these are law students rather than graduates) or a clerk of court (an administrator of the court in question). Universally, attorneys and judges agree that a judicial clerkship is one of the most prestigious and competitive positions you can secure. See also Chapter Twelve: Internships and Externships.

While the responsibilities of a judicial clerk may vary from one court to the next, they generally include researching and analyzing pending cases, drafting memoranda containing recommendations (also known as "bench memoranda"), assisting the judge with hearings and trials, drafting opinions, proofreading opinions, and cite-checking opinions.

TYPES OF COURT

In the United States, there are judicial clerkships available in:

 State trial courts

 State appellate courts

 State supreme courts

 Specialty federal courts such as bankruptcy and tax courts

 Federal district courts, federal appellate courts

 The Supreme Court of the United States

STATE COURTS (TRIAL, APPELLATE, SUPREME)

These courts exist to contribute to the development of state common law and interpret state statute, which has a resounding impact on state law. These courts handle civil and criminal matters that are heard first through the trial courts, then appellate courts and/or the supreme court. Students interested in criminal law should consider a judicial internship in a state trial court as this will provide the best insight into trial proceedings.

SPECIALTY FEDERAL COURTS

Judicial clerks and interns at bankruptcy courts are responsible for drafting memoranda and reviewing cases related to bankruptcy law. Judicial clerks also answer attorney questions regarding court procedures and policies. In tax courts, you can expect to observe cases that may include income, gift taxes, and estate issues. If you are interested in a clerkship or internship in the Tax Court, consider taking and achieving high marks in tax law courses. An undergraduate major in accounting is also very helpful and shows demonstrated interest. The Court of International Trade is a another specialty court that has a nationwide jurisdiction arising out of customs and international trade law of the United States.

FEDERAL COURTS

Positions in federal courts, regardless of the court , are extremely competitive. There are 94 federal districts in the United States with either a district or a magistrate judge. Applications for federal judicial clerkships open in early September in deference to the Federal Hiring Plan.

Students seeking these positions should prepare applications the summer before their third year for submission by the September deadline. Preparing your applications starting in June or July of the summer before your third year is crucial due to the 14-day application period. The process moves quickly so preparation is key.

THE SUPREME COURT OF THE UNITED STATES

These are the most competitive positions and the experience is invaluable. While the Supreme Court is a federal court, it is worth noting the special requirements as this is the hardest position to secure. As a clerk, you will read and attend oral arguments. Most applicants and considerations are for those who have completed a federal appellate clerkship. If this is your aim, you may also consider vying for a clerkship at the Court of Appeals for the District of Colombia Circuit courts. The justices determine their own hiring schedule so periodically check for announcements well in advance of application. It is important to note that these positions are so presitigious that clerks at the end of their term are aggressively recruited by major firms and are even offered signing bonuses! In addition to job opportunities in big law, Supreme Court clerks are highly sought after in academia as well.

★ most competitive

★ extremely competitive

★ very competitive

★ competitive

ADVANTAGES AND DISADVANTAGES

The best way to learn about a judicial clerkship and whether it is the right choice for you is to work as a judicial extern or judicial intern during your legal studies. As a judicial extern, you will have the opportunity to work closely with a judge and law clerk(s) and gain practical insight into the inner working of a judge's chambers.

ADVANTAGES

EXPANDED RESEARCH AND WRITING SKILLS

Not only will a judicial clerkship provide you with practical legal skills, but you may also gain a mentor. Your substantive knowledge of the law, research skills, writing skills, and oral argument and presentation skills will be enhanced. The opportunity to observe the written work and courtroom conduct of other lawyers is invaluable. It will give you insight into what judges find persuasive, what they ignore, and importantly what judges dislike.

PROFESSIONAL DEVELOPMENT AND PERSPECTIVE

Not sure if you want to be a trial or appellate lawyer? Judicial clerkships are invaluable in that they provide experience into specific practice areas, even whether you would like to work in a courtroom. By the time you accept your first position, you will have the skills and experience to be "courtroom ready!"

RESUME BOOST!

The skills and experience you gain through a judicial clerkship help you stand out from your peers. Large firms usually allow their new associates to delay their start date by up to two years if they secured a judicial clerkship position.

> "Time spent in the judge's chambers has been my best training. I was educated on substantive issues and stylistic habits that I now use in practice. Most importantly, I was able to build a relationship with the judge that opened up many career opportunities that I would not otherwise have."

Kristine Santos, Class of 2019

DISADVANTAGES

SALARY

The average starting salary for judicial clerks is $66,050. This is about half of the median starting salary of new associates at large firms. Given the debt that law students incur during law school, this salary may seem hard to accept. However, this salary is comparable to the salaries of entry-level associates at small to medium-sized law firms.

SHORT-TERM POSITION

As mentioned before, judicial clerkships are termed positions that last up to two years. This means that those interested in working as judicial clerks will be on the job hunt and sometimes after only one year. (Don't forget that the resume value may aid in securing a position faster than usual). Another disadvantage of the position is that start and end dates are usually inflexible and hours and commitment are established during the offer process.

CLERKSHIP REQUIREMENTS

Are clerkships only available to students who attend tier-one law schools? The answer is "No." There are many clerkships available, and they are open to all, provided applicants meet the requirements. While the most prestigious clerkships (those in federal courts and the United States Supreme Court) are extremely competitive and are most often secured by students and graduates from top-tier schools, all positions require rigorous academic credentials. Yes, class rank and GPA are essential factors in meeting minimum requirements.

If your grades are not as competitive as you'd like, consider working as a judicial extern to beef up your resume. Proving you can do the job may give you the edge you need. If you do well in your position, your judge may serve as a referencer for you. Memberships on a school-sanctioned legal journal such as law review or moot court teams are also valued.

Finally, to work as a federal judicial clerk in the United States, you must be one of the following: 1) A United States citizen; 2) A person who owes allegiance to the U.S. (as described in 8 U.S.C. 1408); 3) A refugee, or someone granted asylum, who has filed a declaration of intention to become a lawful permanent resident and then a citizen when eligible, or 4) A lawful permanent resident who is seeking citizenship as outlined in 8 U.S.C. 1324b(a)(3)(B).

WHERE TO APPLY
State courts
★ State trial courts
★ State appellate courts
★ State specialty courts

Federal courts
★ Federal magistrate courts
★ Federal specialty courts
★ Federal district courts
★ Federal appellate courts
★ Supreme Court of the United States

WHEN TO APPLY
After you have researched where and for whom you would like to clerk, you should apply in the early fall of your last year of law school. If you are successful, your clerkship position will begin in the fall after your graduation or at the beginning of the next clerkship term. Check application deadlines, as they may vary. Apply only to those positions for which you would accept a clerkship, and send applications in waves to avoid having to decline an interview or offer.

Pro tips

DEADLINES

Because application deadlines vary, begin checking both state and federal court due dates during your second year of law school.

"Working as a judicial clerk can lead you to qualify for higher starting salaries or clerkship bonuses due to your experience."

COMPLETING YOUR APPLICATION

Begin preparing your application materials during your second year of legal studies (if you are a part-time student, begin at the start of your third-year). You will need a cover letter, resume, updated official or unofficial transcript (requirements vary so carefully read the guidelines), a writing sample, and letters of recommendation.

COVER LETTER

Follow the formatting for the cover letter discussed on pages 140–141 and apply the following:

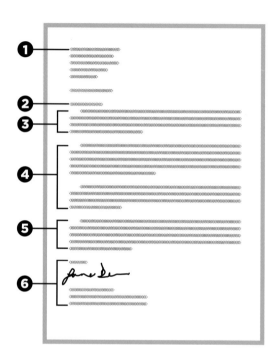

1 **Recipient's address**: Properly address the judge/justice—for example, "The Honorable Jane Doe" or "The Honorable Jane Doe, Magistrate Judge" (Federal Courts). Add the date on a new line.

2 **Salutation**: "Dear Justice Doe" (U.S. Supreme Court and State Supreme and some Appellate Court Justices); "Dear Judge Doe" (all other judges)

3 **First paragraph**: State the clerkship term to which you are applying, and briefly share with the judge why you want to be their law clerk. Use this as an opportunity to name drop, and mention any person you have a connection with, who might help influence your application. For example, you may write: "This past summer, I had the privilege of working for the Honorable Madeleine R. Banks, magistrate judge for the United States District Court for the Central District of California."

4 **Second and third paragraphs**: Provide reasons and evidence as to why you are a good fit for the position.

5 **Closing paragraph**: If you are relocating, consider briefly sharing your plans. You can say something like "I am very interested in this clerkship as I intend to move back to Washington and continue my professional career in the state."

6 **Sign-off**: Use "Sincerely." Add your signature to the document and, below it, type your name as it appears on your letterhead. Type your class year below that, and then your email address.

RESUME

Format your resume according to the sample discussed on pages 138–139. To make your judicial clerkship resume focused, consider the following:

 Free of errors: Review your resume to confirm that there are no errors. Submitting a resume for a judicial clerkship that has any errors is the easiest way to ensure your application is rejected.

 Class rank or GPA: The assumption is that if you are applying to a judicial clerkship, you have a competitive GPA. However, if you feel your GPA is not competitive, and listing your GPA is not a requirement, you are not obligated to list it on your resume.

 Research and writing skills: Highlighting these skills in your resume and expounding upon your experience in this area is helpful. Remember this is what you will be doing as a judicial clerk.

Writing sample

★ Carefully read and follow the guidelines for the position. If the job listing states that you must submit a writing sample that is more than three pages but less than ten, do as they ask. Note that any sample you send must be your own work.

★ If you are submitting a document you drafted for work, get permission from your employer and make sure that all confidential information has been redacted. This is especially true if submitting bench memoranda or other documents written for a judge.

★ Transcripts: This bears repeating. Order an unofficial copy of your transcript. Order an official copy if required.

Pro tips

LETTERS OF RECOMMENDATION

Judges usually require two to three letters of recommendation. Be prepared to ask your supervising attorney, professor, or even the judge for your judicial externship to write a letter for you. If you can prepare ahead of time, you will give your recommender enough time to write a meaningful recommendation for you.

THE INTERVIEW

You did it! You received an interview for a prestigious position and it seems like all your hard work has paid off! Not quite. Now is the time for you to pore over your applications to make sure you know them inside and out. You should prepare for a judicial clerkship interview the same way you prepare for other interviews.

RESEARCH

Research the court, the judge's background, and opinions as well as the jurisdiction. You should also know how many judges sit on the court, what type of cases the court hears, who the chief judge or justice is, and so on. You may also want to briefly review the rules of court in the jurisdiction. Contact people you know who have worked for the judge. Do not assume that judges decide cases based on political persuasion, regardless of whether they authored an opinion on a controversial matter.

Commonly asked interview questions

★ Why do you want to do a clerkship?

★ Have you applied to other courts? Other types of courts?

★ Have you applied to many judges?

★ What research did you do to prepare for the interview?

★ What aspects of the law interest you most?

★ Why do you think you would be a valuable law clerk?

★ What do you see yourself doing in five years? Ten years?

★ Various questions about your writing sample.

★ If you and I disagreed about a certain issue of a case, would you be able to draft an opinion supporting my viewpoint?

★ Why did you [or not] do a judicial externship?

★ Tell me about your judicial externship.

PREPARE QUESTIONS FOR THE JUDGE OR LAW CLERK

As well as preparing for the questions that will be asked of you, you will also need to contemplate your own questions. Make sure that these are genuine and pertain to the position.

THANK-YOU LETTERS

Refer to the section on thank-you letters (see page 127). Be sure to make all your thank-you letters unique and sincere and send them as soon as possible.

JOB OFFER

Congratulations! You received an offer for a highly competitive judicial clerkship. After you do your happy dance, remember to do the following:

Respond ASAP: You are expected to respond to a judicial clerkship offer on the spot or within twenty-four hours of receipt of the offer. If a judge states that you may consider an offer for longer, the unwritten rule is you should make your decision within twenty-four hours. You can also request twenty-four hours if no time frame for acceptance is given (or if the offer is supposed to be answered on the spot and you feel unable to do so).

Adhere to deadlines: Precisely follow any time deadlines and/or any requirements that you accept or decline in writing. Once you accept an offer, you will be expected to honor it. Failing to honor an offer may harm your ability to obtain other clerkships as the judicial community is small. Finally, your conduct could stifle the chances of other students from your school who will apply in the future.

CHAPTER FOURTEEN

WORKING PRO BONO

All lawyers are encouraged to take on cases to help people who would otherwise be unable to afford legal services. There are many personal and professional benefits to working pro bono.

While the legal profession can be very lucrative, it also has a human, community-centered tradition of contributing to the public good. In Europe, pro bono counsel can be traced back to 15th-century British law; in the Americas it has existed since the 1770s, before the founding of the United States. Every year, countries worldwide participate in Public Interest Week, where lawyers and students come together to offer pro bono services locally, nationally, and internationally. Providing access to justice is the backbone of pro bono efforts, and lawyers from small to large firms participate in this public service enthusiastically.

Law students can benefit from public interest organizations and law firms that offer pro bono services. Whether they are working for a law firm or public interest organization, law students who participate in pro bono activities, under an attorney's supervision, stand to gain relevant transferable legal skills while working with a diverse population.

Giving back to the community can be one of the most rewarding aspects of being a lawyer. Moreover, it can take various forms, from providing legal aid for low-income families to representing small nonprofits or simply helping out on a hotline. This chapter discusses the different types of pro bono work and outlines opportunities for participation.

WHY WORK PRO BONO?

There are many personal and professional benefits to working pro bono. Whether you choose to do so because you have a passion for your community or because you have a passion for a specific practice area, providing free legal assistance benefits all those involved.

 ### HELP YOUR COMMUNITY

For many lawyers, working pro bono may be a passion to which they devote their entire professional life or a tangible outlet for those seeking to connect with their community outside of fee services. Pro bono attorneys largely agree that the most important benefit of working pro bono is to be a resource to the community while offsetting the high cost of skilled legal assistance. The presence of pro bono attorneys and public-interest organizations is proof that public legal assistance is lacking. Attorneys who work pro bono use their legal knowledge to fill the gap created by society.

 ### HONE PRACTICAL LAWYERING SKILLS

Freshly minted lawyers can expound upon the skills they gained during their legal studies and through on-the-job training through working pro bono. As a new attorney, you have the opportunity to work directly with seasoned attorneys (some of whom may be partners at prestigious law firms and public-interest organizations). For example, you can test your knowledge through honing skills such as client-management and oral advocacy. The ability to successfully communicate with, and for, clients from various socio-economic backgrounds is a wonderful skill to add to your professional development toolbox. In any legal position, gaining practical legal skills is a great way to add depth and demonstrated interest in application materials.

 ### ENHANCING YOUR FIRM'S REPUTATION

Believe it or not, firms encourage their attorneys to work on pro bono cases; even going so far as to provide billable credit for volunteering. Why do they do this? Donating time to pro bono cases is a win for all involved. A client receives the free assistance they need and firms can prove their commitment to the community-at-large while developing their attorneys.

 ### INCREASE YOUR PROFESSIONAL NETWORK

Have you heard the saying, "great minds think alike?" Working pro bono with other legal professionals is like a meeting of the minds where you have a chance to work with other legal professionals who are as passionate as you. For example, some organizations are led by retired appellate court justices and some national public interest organizations are chaired by partners in major international law firms.

Pro bono *(adjective)*
\ ˌprō-bō-(ˌ)nō \:being, involving, or doing professional and especially legal work donated especially for the public good. *(Merriam-Webster)*

What does pro bono mean to law students?

How do employers view unpaid positions?

Are they taken seriously?

Where does working pro bono at a law firm fit in your career plan?

In your second semester of law school, you may begin hearing the terms "volunteer law clerk" or "pro bono clinic law clerk" from your professors, career advisors, or even upper-class students. In addition to working as paid law clerks, students can volunteer their time to assist clients in many different practice areas.

First-year law students typically begin their first pro bono position in the summer before their second year. The question that plagues every law student considering working pro bono is "How do employers view unpaid positions?" and "Are they taken seriously?" In the

hierarchy of positions, judicial externships and post-graduate judicial clerkships are the most coveted and prestigious positions. So, where does volunteering for a pro bono organization or working pro bono at a law firm fit in your career plan?

The answer to this question depends upon your personal goals. Suppose you know you want to work in immigration law, and there are many immigration law firms and clinics available to hone your skills. Why not choose the position that will allow you the most opportunity to gain practical legal skills while realizing a life-long passion?

PRO BONO OPPORTUNITIES

From family law to environmental law, the opportunity to work in pro bono is vast. There are more than a few ways to work in pro bono and this next section will discuss how to gain legal experience while working in your passion. While reviewing these opportunities, be sure to research the employer's portfolio as it pertains to their commitment to pro bono. Is there an established pro bono program? Is there demonstrated dedication assisting the underserved? What sort of cases have they tried and won? Seeking answers to these questions can help you determine personal and professional fit.

EXTERNSHIPS AND INTERNSHIPS

Externships and internships are productive ways to gain legal experience; they are also a vehicle by which students can network with other legal professionals. Participating in a pro bono externship or internship offers the same benefits without the pay. Externships/internships/unpaid work placements are offered at all public interest organizations and many law firms with pro bono committees. They can be found through your university or online. See also Chapter Twelve: Internships and Externships.

Before you write off the entire experience because of the lack of payment, consider the following benefits:

You can work in virtually any practice area and create long-lasting professional relationships with practicing attorneys.

Working pro bono shows passion and demonstrated interest in a practice area and provides relevant work experience.

Students can extern/intern working in the public interest in government agencies, local and national organizations, and even law firms!

You get to speak with clients to help facilitate change.

FELLOWSHIPS

Large firms and public interest organizations will sponsor a fellow, or fellows, to work in the public interest for the summer (for students) or one to two years after graduation. While fellowships differ from traditional pro bono positions, they are unique in that fellows may never work for the firm in which they are sponsored.

Conversely, fellows may work entirely for firms on designated pro bono projects. It is important to note that while legal fellows do not work strictly pro bono, they are sometimes paid substantially less than their counterparts who charge a fee for legal services. Students and recent graduates can obtain fellowships all over the world, working in virtually any practice area. There are two types of fellowships: project-based and organization-based.

PROJECT-BASED FELLOWSHIPS

These are fellowships that are generally funded by a third party. For example, a student wants to create and run a project assisting asylees. A separate public interest organization is looking for someone who wants to establish a practice focused on asylee rights and information. The student and the organization would then work together to apply for the fellowship and subsequent fellowship funding organization from a third-party such as a law firm.

ORGANIZATION-BASED FELLOWSHIPS

These are fellowships that are available directly through the funding organization. National and international public interest organizations offer fellowships annually.

Pro tips

BE AN EARLY BIRD

Regardless of the type, fellowships are extremely competitive. If you are interested in applying, talk to your career advisor and start the process early. According to Equal Justice Works, an internationally recognized organization dedicated to the advancement of legal public service, the process from application to start date for personally designed fellowships can take as long as one year.

PROGRAMS WITHIN FIRMS

Many firms have established pro bono programs that are filled with their associates. Why do these multi-million dollar firms choose to spend time and resources on public service? The answer is simple: They feel a special responsibility to use their practiced knowledge for the good of the community.

While they should be commended for using their talents for good, there are benefits for firms who encourage their associates to volunteer their time. First, law firms who encourage and have an established commitment to public service attract passionate lawyers. These are the individuals who joined the profession seeking to help their community. When a firm allows an associate, especially a new associate, to take the lead on a case they are placing value on personal goals.

LARGE FIRMS

Second, providing pro bono opportunities in large firms allows associates to enhance their skills. In a pro bono setting, they may be able to communicate with clients or even litigate a trial, allowing for a break in the day-to-day monotony of document review. Law students may also find pro bono opportunities in law firms. The opportunity to assist with litigating a case or drafting various documents serves as a resume-boosting experience while enhancing professional competencies.

SMALL FIRMS AND TRANSACTIONAL WORK

Suppose you are not interested in becoming a litigator. In that case, there are opportunities to provide pro bono assistance in various practice areas such as intellectual property, tax, mergers and acquisitions, and real estate, to name a few. There are benefits to transactional pro bono work as well:

★ Transactional lawyers can be activists. For example, a transactional lawyer can work on economic justice-related projects as well as entertainment or business contracts and leases.

★ Working for a transactional law clinic through your school or an organization can provide you with relevant hard skills such as legal analysis, client interviewing, and contract drafting and negotiations. The opportunity to hone soft skills, such as attention to detail, business expertise, and project management, is also prevalent in these positions. See also Chapter Eight: After the Race.

CORPORATIONS

Is it your goal to work for a corporation as in-house counsel? While the road to in-house counsel may be long and bumpy, you can start your law school career by volunteering with an actual in-house counsel. Recently, companies have begun encouraging volunteerism. Law firms and companies alike have found that encouraging volunteering not only increases company morale, it also increases public knowledge. A simple Internet search of corporations who partner with local public interest organizations will provide you with available opportunities and more insight into how corporations are working with the public to help deliver social justice.

Other avenues

Some lawyers and law students prefer to use their skills to help their community in real time. Some may volunteer their time to conduct workshops and training on civil and immigrants' rights. Street Law, Inc. is a global nonprofit organization that educates young people on law and government through classroom and community programming. Other attorneys volunteer their time through participating in legal hotlines or pop-up clinics designed to help individuals with general legal advice.

"I tell law students . . . if you are going to be a lawyer and just practice your profession, you have a skill—very much like a plumber. But if you want to be a true professional, you will do something outside yourself . . . something that makes life a little better for people less fortunate than you."

Supreme Court Justice Ruth Bader Ginsburg

PROFESSIONAL PRO BONO ORGANIZATIONS

Pro bono opportunities are far and wide. If you seek to be an attorney who specializes in the public interest or would like to volunteer your time, consider joining a professional organization to make connections, and gain more insight into the pro bono arena. For example, you can join the National Association of Pro Bono Professionals in the United States. This organization focuses on bringing together attorneys who are interested in advocating for the poor and disenfranchised. In addition to national organizations, you can also join a local bar association. Many bar associations offer students and recent graduates discounted membership, so take advantage. Once you join an association, look for pro bono or practice-area-specific sections so you can meet and network with those professionals.

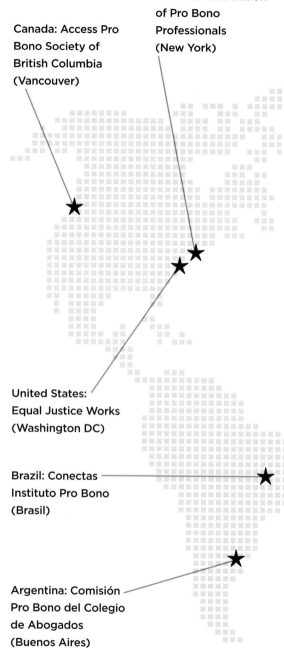

Canada: Access Pro Bono Society of British Columbia (Vancouver)

United States: National Association of Pro Bono Professionals (New York)

United States: Equal Justice Works (Washington DC)

Brazil: Conectas Instituto Pro Bono (Brasil)

Argentina: Comisión Pro Bono del Colegio de Abogados (Buenos Aires)

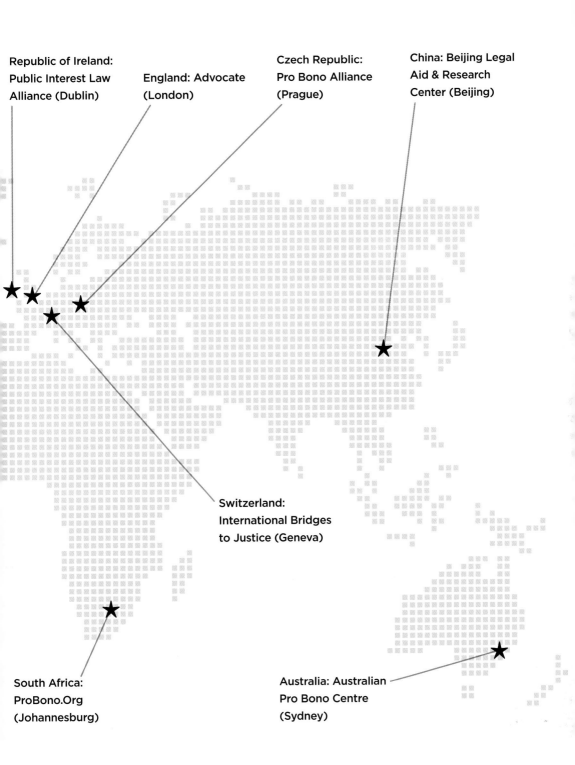

Republic of Ireland:
Public Interest Law
Alliance (Dublin)

England: Advocate
(London)

Czech Republic:
Pro Bono Alliance
(Prague)

China: Beijing Legal
Aid & Research
Center (Beijing)

Switzerland:
International Bridges
to Justice (Geneva)

South Africa:
ProBono.Org
(Johannesburg)

Australia: Australian
Pro Bono Centre
(Sydney)

CHAPTER FIFTEEN

TAKING CARE OF YOURSELF

Once you graduate from law school and take any examination in your jurisdiction to be licensed to practice law, you will officially be a lawyer. It is a wonderful feeling! While being a lawyer can be extremely rewarding, as you will have gained tools and skills to help people with simple and complex legal issues, being a lawyer can also take over your life, which can quickly lead to burnout.

Because the training involved in becoming a lawyer is so intense, many who are driven to work in this profession are generally high-achieving individuals who strive for excellence. This is certainly not a bad quality, but oftentimes these same individuals (or the organizations they work for) are under immense pressure to perform at exceptionally high levels, often to the detriment of their health, mental well-being, and family time.

This is not meant to discourage you from becoming a lawyer; being a lawyer is a very noble career! But, given that the law touches nearly every aspect of our lives, it is no wonder that lawyers are an important and indispensable part of our society. And it is because of their importance that lawyers must be vigilant in self-care.

This chapter introduces tips and techniques for building a daily practice of protecting your mental, physical, emotional, and spiritual health while you are in law school. By building this practice early, you can maintain these habits as you begin your legal practice. Specifically, this section provides insight into managing the stressors of law school, such as accessing the mental health resources your law school offers, as well as including regular exercise, rest, and play into your schedule. Think of law school as a high-intensity job; you need to take care of yourself to be able to do it well.

DEALING WITH THE STRESSES OF LAW SCHOOL

Law school is a different world than the undergraduate experience of most students. The stress of law school can be due to the curricular format of many law schools that rely on a single (or very few) final assessment products, such as an exam or paper that determines your entire grade for the course. Also, like many professional schools, law school draws the best and brightest through its doors. So, the competition is tough.

While a healthy amount of stress can be motivating at times, too much that lasts for too long is not good and can lead to mental, physical, emotional, and spiritual discouragement. Being aware of your stress is healthy, as is getting help to deal with stress in healthy ways. Many law schools have dedicated resources to help with student well-being. They may include mindful meditation, therapy animals, individual/group counseling, and even law school courses dedicated to well-being.

COUNSELING

As humans we are complex and thoughtful beings, but despite our best intentions to always think positively and confidently about ourselves and the world around us, we struggle and our actions on the outside do not always align with our thoughts on the inside. So, we can become anxious, depressed, and frustrated at any inability to "fix" our own thoughts. Law students, in particular, are prone to anxiety, as well as self-defeating and impostor syndrome thoughts (see pages 194–195).

You should know that the core of your thoughts may flow from the heart. So, sometimes, good mental health and well-being start with getting to the "heart of an issue" so that you can gain tools to better understand or correct your thoughts and actions. Therapists and counselors are experienced professionals that can help explore the root causes of unhealthy thinking and behaviors.

JOURNALING

Journaling, the process of writing down your fears and joys, is a wonderful medium of self-care that can alleviate stress. As you learn to become a lawyer you will experience many emotions along the way—anxiety and fear, but also joy and accomplishment. Such moments are an important part of becoming a lawyer, and should be not be overlooked.

By writing down how you feel, you can prioritize fears and problems, manage the endless to-do lists that flow through your mind, capture the high moments of your day, while letting go of low points. Try "bullet journaling," where you jot down your personal goals, daily activities, and intimate thoughts in a fun and artistic way.

Mindful meditation

There are many ways to practice mindfulness in your daily life, whether through spiritual prayer, guided meditation, or yoga, all of which allow you to practice being present.

Here are some tips for guided meditation:

★ Find a quiet place where you won't be disturbed.

★ Sit comfortably with your feet firmly planted on the floor.

★ Set a timer for 5 to 10 minutes.

★ If you have a spiritual practice, begin your time with a short prayer.

★ Focus on observing your breath.

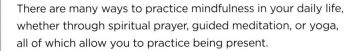

Close your eyes and inhale deeply through the nose for 5 to 10 seconds, letting your chest fill with air . . .

holding it . . .

and then exhaling with your mouth open for 5 to 10 seconds.

★ Let thoughts come and go, neither pursuing them nor pushing them away.

★ When you realize you've gotten distracted, bring your attention back to your breath.

★ Keep going until the timer goes off.

★ Do it again tomorrow. And the next day.

A HEALTHY LIFESTYLE

Your time in law school will place an incredible amount of stress on your body—mentally, emotionally, and physically. It is imperative, therefore, that you keep your body operating at its optimum in terms of health. That means taking good exercise, diet, and sleep seriously.

EXERCISE

Exercise releases endorphins in your body, which are your brain's feel-good neurotransmitters. And when you feel good, the effects of stress are greatly minimized! If you already had a regular exercise routine prior to law school—keep doing it! If you did not have one, it is not too late to start. If you are concerned about how much exercise you should try, consult your doctor. Here are some things to do:

★ Take daily walks (around the block, up some stairs)
★ Swim some lengths of a pool
★ Go dancing
★ Join a yoga/pilates/tai chi class

DIET

What good is exercise for your body if you go to the kitchen and "fuel" it with unhealthy items? Would you put toxins or dangerous chemicals in your car and expect it to perform at its highest level? Of course not! Your body is the same—even more so in law school, when you need to perform at your highest level. There are endless tips on the best foods for energy, how much water you should consume daily, and natural products to boost concentration and productivity. Here are three to start you off:

★ Conduct an online search for guidelines on good nutrition and a balanced diet.
★ Follow the recommended guidelines for how much water you should be drinking in a day.
★ Consider using essential oils for productivity and focus.

Just Getting Started Exercises for Law Students

★ Daily walks (around the block, up some stairs)

★ Swimming lengths of a pool

★ Biking

★ Dancing

★ Yoga/Pilates/Tai Chi

★ Jogging

De-stressing your body

Brain: Seek counseling for substance use and mental health concerns. Practice meditation.

Eyes: Give your eyes a break from constant reading. Look at things that make you laugh.

Nose: Get some fresh air daily.

Mouth: Communicate with your family and pre-law school friends. It is healthy to have nonlaw outlets to speak with and stay connected with the rest of the world. Smile, often. Breathe.

Ears: Listen to positive music.

Shoulders: You cannot carry the weight of law school alone. Reach out to mentors to stay encouraged.

Body: Keep yourself in shape. Shower, get regular exercise (walking, yoga, and so on), so that you can be physically prepared for the rigors of law school.

Hands: Write down to-do lists, so that you can manage your time wisely.

Legs: Be mindful when you've been sitting too long; take short walks around the block or stretch in your home.

Feet: Stay grounded in the present moment; while law school will present a challenge, it is doable and you can do it!

SLEEP

College students sleep around 6 hours a day on average, despite the recommendation for this age group to be between 7 and 9 hours. As a law student, getting regular and healthful sleep is important for strong academic performance because it affects recall, concentration, and alertness. Here are some tips for a good night's sleep:

★ Set a bedtime that allows for a minimum of 7 hours sleep.
★ Avoid stimulants and heavy foods before bed (caffeine, nicotine).
★ Turn off the screen (television, computer, phone) at least 15 to 30 minutes before bed.
★ Do a yoga flow or meditation practice prior to bedtime.
★ Have a clean and designated space for sleeping.
★ Place a diffuser in your sleep space for aromatherapy benefits and diffuse calming oils (lavender, cedarwood).

CHAPTER SIXTEEN

DIVERSITY, INCLUSION, AND EQUITY

Take a jaunt through legal history, and two broad points emerge: first, lawyers have long played a social role—at times ambiguous and even detestable, but often emerging as prominent and respected; and second, this role was usually cast by publicly elite men. This system goes back to the Roman Empire, when a distinct group of men, known as orators, obtained legal training to act as advocates on behalf of those who did not want to speak for themselves.

The Roman pattern of legal organization influenced Europe in large measure and spread to other countries through colonization. Fast forward several centuries, and it is the demographics of the legal profession that have seen, and needed, the most change. For example, in the United States, even as late as the mid-20th century, few women and ethnic minorities attended law school, and while there have been some upward shifts in this trend, the disparity, particularly on ethnicity, is glaring. For this reason, a discussion about diversity in the legal profession is paramount.

We all benefit from being in diverse, inclusive, and equitable environments. Such environments are integral to you getting the most out of your study of law and the law school experience. Research has shown that diverse, inclusive, and equitable work and educational spaces encourage innovation, productivity, problem-solving, and decision-making. Unfortunately, most organizations still have a long way to go. Using the United States as a case study, this chapter discusses how to recognize and deal with bias, manage impostor syndrome and stereotype threat, and build ally networks. Developing strategies to confront bias and discrimination will give you better tools to navigate difficult situations in law school and make progress and success possible.

THE UNITED STATES AS A CASE STUDY

After the United States gained its independence from Great Britain, the nation's Founding Fathers determined that no free society could exist without a legal system.

During the country's fight for independence, the term "white," referring to a "race," began to be used to distinguish the light-skinned Protestant English-speakers from the brown-skinned Native and indigenous people whom they displaced. Even though "white" was a made-up term without meaning, because the nation's historical legal documents—the Declaration of Independence and the U.S. Constitution— were drafted by "white" men, many of whom were lawyers and slaveholders, those who looked "white" gained significant power and priority. And so began America's racial history.

The pattern of legal organization begun by Rome later influenced nearly every country that established some form of legal system. Those who were advocates received special university training, and such training was not available to women or people of color, who did not even enter the profession until the mid-20th century and later.

ETHNIC IMPARTIALITY

Diversity, inclusion, and equity are each distinct and equally important in moving toward the lofty goal of ethnic impartiality. Diversity alone is not enough.

"Diversity is being asked to the party. Inclusion is being asked to dance."

Verna Myers, inclusion strategist

Diversity:
Differences among people in terms of their race/ethnicity, socioeconomic background, geography, religion/spirituality, political beliefs, sexual orientation, gender, life experience, and so on.

Currently, the demographics for women and people of color have greatly increased, but the seismic advantage that males, particularly white males, had in establishing the profession is still evident in the lack of diversity in the broader legal profession. Nearly 200 years later, the American legal profession is still not very diverse. The American Bar Association (ABA), a voluntary organization of lawyers and law students founded in 1878, reported that, as of 2020, the legal profession in the United States is comprised of 86% white people, 63% males, and 37% females.

"Our mission is to serve equally our members, our profession, and the public by defending liberty and delivering justice as the national representative of the legal profession."

The American Bar Association

Given these statistics, how can the American legal profession serve equally when it does not reflect equally the public it is intended to serve? This imbalance is why diversity, inclusion, and equity are so important in the legal profession. Lawyers must reflect the citizens they serve.

Inclusion:

Concerns whether a person feels valued or welcomed in an organization. Inclusion has to be intentional, as it is not a natural byproduct of visible diversity.

Equity:

The process or approach by which an organization provides access to the same opportunities to all of its members. Approaches to ensuring access may be different for majority and minority groups. Like inclusion, equity has to be intentional, and borne from education about the fact that members of minority groups have historically been underrepresented in the legal profession.

Bias is simply the preference of one thing over another (such as preferring coffee over tea). It can be either positive or negative. In other words, our brains rely on categorization as a fundamental tool. In relationships, however, any tendency to believe that certain social groups are better than others can result in some people being treated unfairly.

EXPLICIT AND IMPLICIT BIAS

Explicit bias refers to attitudes and beliefs that we consciously or deliberately hold and express. Conversely, implicit bias refers to the attitudes and beliefs that we are not aware of, and these behaviors can even contradict what we explicitly believe.

Interest in implicit bias has grown for two main reasons: First, it challenges traditional notions of our cognitive process—that attitudes and stereotypes are always conscious; second, social psychologists have documented a prevalence of unconscious racial bias that sadly indicates implicit anti-Black bias across all ethnic identities.

However, implicit or unconscious bias is very controversial because some question any link between unconscious bias and discriminatory behavior, while others suggest seeking purity and precision from science in this area stalls forward movement on a complex social problem.

The Implicit Association Test

The most popular test that attempts to measure implicit biases is the Implicit Association Test (IAT), developed by Anthony Greenwald (University of Washington) and Mahzarin Banaji (Harvard University). The IAT is a computer-based test that asks participants to associate words (positive or negative) with certain images and scores response time. You can take the test at: https://implicit.harvard.edu/implicit/takeatest.html.

Some people have critiqued the IAT for lack of a causal relationship between the reaction time and bias, or for focusing on biases at the individual instead of institutional level. Despite critiques of the IAT in terms of its effectiveness in measuring bias, scholars generally agree to the existence of unconscious bias and do support its role in starting the conversation about the science of bias.

Stereotype:
Viewing Asian Americans as the "model minority"—high-achieving, assimilated into American society.

Unconscious bias:
Confusing the names of one African American woman for another African American woman when the two are not similar in appearance.

Pre-judging:
Believing that an entry-level female attorney will not want to be on the partnership track at the law firm because at some point she will want to start a family.

Behavior:
Consistently offering assistance to a person who has a disability without first asking if they would like help.

Discrimination:
Not providing a male attorney with quality law firm assignments after he makes it known that he is gay.

STRATEGIES FOR DISRUPTING BIAS

If there is some science behind our unconscious behaviors negatively impacting a particular group, then even our best conscious efforts may not ensure we will always treat others fairly, especially when we make quick decisions, are unfamiliar with a particular group/culture, or find ourselves in a new setting. Instead, our unconscious behaviors may become our default frame of reference and preference.

Recognizing and disrupting bias is not easy, but it is not impossible either. To start, we must slow down and step out of our comfort zone. Here are some strategies:

 BROADEN YOUR SOCIAL SPHERE
Engage in quality interactions with people who are outside your own group (for example, belonging to different racial/ethnic, cultural, social groups) to weaken negative implicit bias. Make efforts to get to know group members as individuals.

 QUESTION YOURSELF
Reflect on why you reacted to someone's behavior in a negative (or biased) way and how that response can be avoided in the future. To move forward we must stop getting defensive toward our own stereotypic thoughts that may produce a negative behavior because then we remain paralyzed and unable to move forward. We are biased, we are imperfect, but we are also intelligent and capable of change. Acknowledge the reaction, assess the truth of that reaction, reflect on a different choice in a similar situation. Move on.

 DOUBT YOUR OBJECTIVITY
Doubt your own objectivity, even when engaging with different viewpoints of your peers. Avoid assuming that their position must be incorrect, and that only your view is right and rational. By nature, humans are biased beings, that is we filter things through categorizations—and often those that are in close proximity to our identity features and preferences—so, we should be cautious in believing that even our very best efforts can render a "neutral" decision.

 LOOK FOR PATTERNS
If you are involved in student organizations where participants discuss and vote on membership, use objective data-keeping to observe whether a pattern of decisions is biased toward one group over another.

"Bias is not something we exhibit and act on all the time. It is conditional, and . . . [a]mong those conditions, speed and ambiguity are two of the strongest triggers of bias."

Jennifer Eberhardt, *Biased* 285 (2019).

"We are biased,
we are imperfect,
but we are
also intelligent
and capable
of change."

IMPOSTOR PHENOMENON

Impostor phenomenon (aka impostor syndrome) refers to the internal experience of intellectual phoniness. It describes the inability of high-achieving people to internalize their success, due to the distorted assumption that they are a phony in their field, despite objective evidence to the contrary.

While people of all gender identities are susceptible to impostor feelings, research indicates that impostor feelings prevent women, more than men, from pursuing goals, owing to familial expectations and gender role socialization. Interestingly, impostor phenomenon sufferers generally do not have low self-esteem, yet they underestimate their own achievements and doubt themselves, while overestimating the strengths of other people. In law school, this might mean that an intelligent law student, who did very well in their undergraduate studies, arrives at law school doubting their own ability to do well, while at the same time, pointing out how smart every other student around them is.

COMBATING IMPOSTOR PHENOMENON

For anyone who may—for reasons of ethnicity, socioeconomic status, family obligations, or others—feel like they do not belong, having mentors to affirm you and validate your intellect and credibility is often a matter of survival in combating impostor phenomenon and succeeding in law school.

"Having just completed my MA in English, graduating at the top of my class, I truly believed that success at law school would come easily to me. However, I soon found out during my first semester that I had severely underestimated the practical and emotional demands of law school. What caught me most by surprise was feeling like a total impostor for the first time in my life, which was largely fueled by the fact that I found myself trying to thrive in a largely white profession. As a woman of color, I can genuinely say that I would have dropped out of law school in my first semester had it not been for the constant mentorship and support from one of my professors—a fellow woman of color—who not only validated my concerns but personally understood the anxiety I was experiencing. Hearing someone say, 'I understand what you're going through,' and actually meaning it, not only kept me in law school but helped me achieve my fullest potential."

Abril Perez, third-year student,
Mexican-American gay woman

SIX CHARACTERISTICS OF IMPOSTOR PHENOMENON

1

The impostor syndrome cycle: A new challenge brings anxiety to overprepare (always) or procrastinate (with any success reduced to sheer luck).

2

The need to be special or the very best: There may be conflict between wanting to be the best, while dismissing your own brilliance.

3

Superwoman/ superman aspects: You may be a perfectionist with ambitious, near-impossible goals.

4

Fear of failure: Your anxiety around failing or making a mistake may lead you to overwork.

5

Denial of competence and discounting praise: You may make an effort to downplay positive feedback.

6

Fear and guilt about success: You may worry about how others will perceive your success.

STEREOTYPE THREAT

A stereotype is an oversimplified—but often widely held—belief about a particular group of people. The term is most often used in connection with unfair or belittling characterizations of a particular group that lead to prejudicial attitudes and result in an "us versus them," or in-group and out-group, mentality. Stereotype threat is when someone feels that they are at risk of confirming a negative stereotype about their social group. Two common stereotype categories are abilities and character.

ABILITY-RELEVANT

This refers to the fear of confirming a stereotype that one's group is less able than other groups to perform a valued activity. In an academic setting, stereotype threat more generally adversely impacts women in STEM fields, and Black and Latino/a students. The "threat" is the student's anxiety over whether a poor performance confirms a stereotype about their group's intellect. The risk to the student: If you remain conscious about the stereotype threat

STRATEGIES FOR COMBATING STEREOTYPE THREAT

SOCIAL BELONGING INTERVENTION

Talk to upper-level students who also felt that they did not belong during their first year, and you will likely find that, for many, those feelings went away after their first year. Knowing this can help protect you from believing that you do not belong when you encounter social adversity.

WISE CRITICISM

It can be difficult, particularly for people of color in a school or work setting, to determine whether negative feedback is a result of bias or whether positive feedback is a form of overpraising on the part of the evaluator to avoid appearing discriminatory.

of perceived lower ability or intellect, you may underperform academically in law school. Moreover, if you do not feel like you belong, you may remain isolated, invisible to your professors, and may fail to reach your fullest academic potential.

CHARACTER-RELEVANT

This describes the worry around whether someone is seen as adhering to prevailing morals or norms. For example, to be racist is generally deemed immoral, and many white people are concerned that they may be seen as racist. The "threat" is whether this concern leads to a desire to avoid perceived racist behavior, which may simply mean avoiding people of color.

The risk to the student: The majority of law professors in U.S. law schools are white. If they are conscious about the threat of being seen as racist, or unfair to a student in any way, they may neglect to provide effective and meaningful feedback or thoughtful career guidance for particular groups of students.

Feeling as though your actions will confirm a negative stereotype about your group is a heavy burden to carry, especially in a new situation like law school. Take steps to combat stereotype threat.

Do not be afraid to ask for specific feedback that is detailed and substantive, to help you grow. In doing so, you can both remove the ambiguity as to the reason for the feedback and gain confidence that the professor believes in you and has high expectations for your progress.

VALUE AFFIRMATION

Continually remind yourself of your broader identity and positive attributes. This is often a hallmark of a strong mentor–mentee relationship.

EMPOWERMENT: TOOLS FOR SUCCESS

Sadly, the reality of bias, impostor phenomenon, and stereotype threat magnify the need for diversity, inclusion, and equity in a profession that has historically struggled, and continues to struggle, with these issues. Naturally, it can feel overwhelming to think about not just how to survive, but how to succeed in law school and the legal profession. But the legal profession needs you! It needs all of your unique identities and viewpoints to better represent society.

It is not enough simply to acknowledge the existence of bias and discrimination. Becoming aware of the trouble spots before you encounter them is empowering, because you will know what to look out for and can equip yourself with the tools to respond in a healthy way.

Empowerment may come externally, through mentorship and ally networks, or internally, through conscious performance of your identity in a way that honors your authentic self.

MENTORS

A mentor is a person, with experience in a certain area, who uses their talent, influence, and wisdom to help another person with fewer developed skills to succeed or grow, usually in some measurable or identifiable way. This is an interpersonal and accountable relationship. Stay open—you may find mentors in unlikely people.

ALLIES

An ally is a person who is not a member of a marginalized group, but who expresses, gives support, or uses their position of power to benefit members of a marginalized group. The ally may provide access (or remove barriers) to that power; they may raise awareness of issues that disproportionally affect marginalized members of a group. Like a mentor, an ally may be found in an unlikely person, but there may not be an interpersonal relationship. An ally could simply be motivated by injustices that affect a particular group.

Why are mentors and allies important?

First, law school is hard. A mentor can hear your concerns and validate your experiences to keep you moving toward your goal of obtaining your law degree. Second, the legal profession is best described as a culture sustained by networks and relationships, so creating an ally network that can champion on your behalf can make you visible in a sea of brilliance.

CONSCIOUS IDENTITY PERFORMANCE

Conscious identity performance is an intentional and thoughtful navigation of your multiple identities. Do you "perform" the various aspects of your identity in a way that is authentic for you, or have you found yourself changing, hiding, or excusing some aspect of yourself in order to fit in? These are tough questions, but ones that it is important to reflect upon.

How you perform or show up to school each day is your choice, but be empowered in making that choice consciously, in full and thoughtful view of the pros and cons. As the legal profession strives toward better representation of the community it serves, the authentic self of every member becomes important because the various facets of your identity bring awareness, inspire dialogue, and promote access into a profession that is desperate for diversity, inclusion, and equity.

"The goal is, first, to intentionally and productively enlighten law students to biases and stereotypes that will confront them, and second, to empower them with both strategic and culturally competent tools to consciously perform their identities in the manner they so choose."

Professor Leslie P. Culver, Esq.

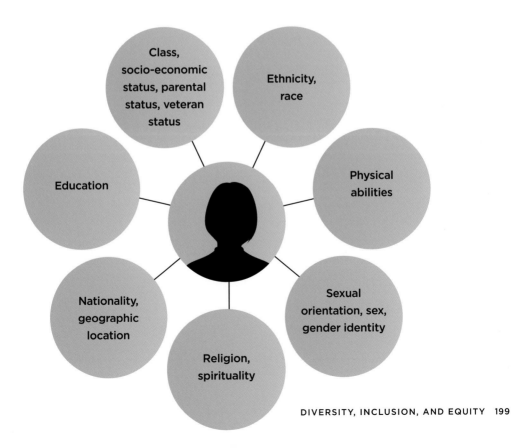

RESOURCES

The samples and templates on the following pages
will help guide you when making important decisions
before, during, and after law school. In some cases, you
can write your entries directly on the pages. To make
the best use of the templates, it is a good idea to make
copies so that you can use them multiple times.

LAW SCHOOL COMPARISON CHART

Law School 1   Address: _____

Contact: _____

Law School 2   Address: _____

Contact: _____

Law School 3   Address: _____

Contact: _____

	Law School 1	Law School 2	Law School 3

APPLICATIONS

	Law School 1	Law School 2	Law School 3
Application fee			
Application due date			
Early admission application date			
Financial aid due date			
Seat deposit due date			
Entrance exam score required			
Undergrad GPA requirement			
Other requirements			

	Law School 1	Law School 2	Law School 3

CURRICULUM

	Law School 1	Law School 2	Law School 3
Concentration areas			
Writing requirements			
Interesting electives			
Dual/joint degree programs			
Available clinics			
Experiential requirements			
Other			

EXTRA/COCURRICULUM ACTIVITIES

	Law School 1	Law School 2	Law School 3
Student organizations of interest			
Career services opportunities			
Law review/journals			
Judicial internships			
Other			

YOUR DEGREE PLAN

Term	Course #	Course name	Credits	Taken	GPA

REQUIRED COURSES

Term	Course #	Course name	Credits	Taken	GPA
Total credits required					

Term	Course #	Course name	Credits	Taken	GPA

ELECTIVES

Total elective credits					
Total credits					

LAW SCHOOL BUDGET

Anticipated Expense	Year	Amount per year
Tuition	1–3	
Student fees	1–3	
Books and course materials	1–3	
Housing	1–3	
Food	1–3	
Health insurance plan (if not included in student fees)	1–3	
Monthly bills (phone, utilities, transportation, etc.)	1–3	
Technology (hardware/software) and subscriptions	1–3	
Application and registration fees for exams, licensing, or certifications	3	
Bar exam review material	3	
Travel during breaks in school	1–3	
Professional clothing	1–3	
Additional costs		
Total	for three years	

BAR EXAM BUDGET

Expense	Amount USD (approx.)
Bar exam application fee	
Moral character application fee	
Registration for the bar exam fee	
Laptop use fee	
Multistate professional responsibility exam	
Exam preparation course	
Housing for three months	
Utilities for three months	
Food for three months	
Car note and insurance for three months	
Smartphone for three months	
Childcare for three months	
Medical bills/health insurance for three months	
Other	
Total	$

WEEKLY STUDY PLAN

Time	Monday	Tuesday	Wednesday	Thursday	Friday	Saturday	Sunday
9:00 → 9:30	Read & brief for Thur. Civil Procedure	Intro to Jurisprudence assignments	Read & brief for Thur. Torts	Update Real Property outline/ study aids	Revise Torts notes	Read & brief for Tues. Contracts	Family time
9:30 → 10:00							
10:00 → 10:30				Real Property practice questions	Update Torts outline		
10:30 → 11:00							
11:00 → 11:30					Torts practice questions		
11:30 → 12:00							
12:00 → 12:30							
12:30 → 13:00		Review Torts notes	Review Intro to Jurisprudence notes	Review Torts notes	Review Intro to Jurisprudence notes		
13:00 → 13:30	Read & brief for Thur. Contract Law	Torts class	Intro to Jurisprudence class	Torts class	Intro to Jurisprudence class	Read & brief for Tues. Torts	
13:30 → 14:00							
14:00 → 14:30			Revise Intro to Jurisprudence notes		Revise Intro to Jurisprudence notes		
14:30 → 15:00		Review Contract Law notes & briefs		Review Contract Law notes & briefs			
15:00 → 15:30	Review Legal Writing notes	Contract Law class	Review ISLM notes	Contract Law class	Read & brief for Mon. Real Property	Update Contract Law outline	
15:30 → 16:00							
16:00 → 16:30	Legal Writing class		Legal Writing class				
16:30 → 17:00		Revise Contract Law notes		Revise Contract Law notes		Contract Law practice questions	
17:00 → 17:30							
17:30 → 18:00							Review briefs for Monday's classes
18:00 → 18:30	Review Real Property notes	Revise Torts notes	Review Real Property notes	Review Civil Procedure notes & briefs		Update Civil Procedure outline	
18:30 → 19:00					Intro to Jurisprudence assignments		
19:00 → 19:30	Real Property class	Read & brief for Wed. Property	Real Property class	Civil Procedure class		Civil Procedure practice questions	
19:30 → 20:00							
20:00 → 20:30							
20:30 → 21:00	Revise Real Property notes and briefs		Revise Real Property notes & briefs				
21:00 → 21:30							

Time	Monday	Tuesday	Wednesday	Thursday	Friday	Saturday	Sunday
9:00 > 9:30							
9:30 > 10:00							
10:00 > 10:30							
10:30 > 11:00							
11:00 > 11:30							
11:30 > 12:00							
12:00 > 12:30							
12:30 > 13:00							
13:00 > 13:30							
13:30 > 14:00							
14:00 > 14:30							
14:30 > 15:00							
15:00 > 15:30							
15:30 > 16:00							
16:00 > 16:30							
16:30 > 17:00							
17:00 > 17:30							
17:30 > 18:00							
18:00 > 18:30							
18:30 > 19:00							
19:00 > 19:30							
19:30 > 20:00							
20:00 > 20:30							
20:30 > 21:00							
21:00 > 21:30							

LEGAL MEMORANDUM TEMPLATE

From

To

Date

Questions presented

Brief answer

Statements of facts

Discussion

Issue or conclusion statement

Rule

Relevant case law

Application of the law to client's facts

Opponent's position

Policy implications

Conclusion

INTERVIEW LOG

JOB TITLE

Name of interviewer(s)

Place of work	Description of role
Date of interview	
Salary	

On the day

Travel arrangements	My "top five"
	1
What to wear	2
	3
Materials to take	4
	5
Questions to ask	

Post Interview

Thank-you letter emailed/posted	Date	Personal note to include
Follow-up letter emailed/posted	Date	

An unsuccessful interview		**A successful interview**	
Rejection letter received	Date	Offer received	Date
Reason for rejection		Offer accepted	Date
		Offer rejected	Date
Next steps		Next steps	

WHY DO I WANT A CAREER IN LAW?

WHO AM I?

_____

_____

_____

WHAT DRIVES ME?

_____

_____

_____

WHAT LIFE EXPERIENCES STAND OUT TO ME?

_____

_____

_____

WHY ARE THEY IMPORTANT?

_____

_____

_____

WHY AM I HERE?

_____

_____

_____

WHY DID I GO TO LAW SCHOOL?

_____

_____

_____

WHY IS STUDYING LAW IMPORTANT TO ME?

_____

_____

_____

WHAT DO I HOPE TO ACHIEVE WITH MY DEGREE?

_____

_____

_____

WHY AM I PURSUING A LEGAL CAREER?

_____

_____

_____

WHAT MAKES ME, ME?

_____

_____

_____

WHAT ARE MY STRENGTHS?

_____

_____

_____

WHAT IS MY PROUDEST ACHIEVEMENT?

_____

_____

_____

WHAT IS MY BIGGEST FAILURE?

_____

_____

_____

WHAT MAKES ME DIFFERENT FROM MY PEERS?

_____

_____

_____

FURTHER READING

BOOKS

LEARNING IN LAW SCHOOL

Brown, Peter C., Henry L. Roediger III, Mark A. McDaniel, *Make It Stick: The Science of Successful Learning*, Harvard University Press, 2014.

Edwards, George E., *LL.M. Roadmap: An International Students Guide to U.S. Law School Programs*, Aspen Publishers Inc., U.S., 2011.

Elder, Dr. Linda and Richard Paul, *Thirty Days to Better Thinking and Better Living Through Critical Thinking*, FT Press, 2012.

Fischl, Richard Michael and Jeremy Paul, *Getting to Maybe: How to Excel on Law School Exams*, 1st edition, 1999.

Franzese, Paula, *A Short & Happy Guide to Being a Law Student 1st Edition*, West Academic Publishing, 2014.

McClurg, Andrew, *1L of a Ride: A Well-traveled Professor's Roadmap to Success in the First Year of Law School*, West Academic Publishing, 2017.

McKinney, Ruth Ann, *Reading Like a Lawyer: Time Saving Strategies for Reading Law Like an Expert*, Carolina Academic Press, 2008.

Miller, Robert H., *Law School Confidential: A Complete Guide to the Law School Experience: By Students, for Students*, St. Martin's Griffin, 2011.

Minsky, Adam S., *The Student Loan Handbook for Law Students and Attorneys*, American Bar Association, 2016.

Stropus, Ruta K. and Charlotte D. Taylor, *Bridging the Gap Between College and Law School: Strategies for Success,* Third Edition, Carolina Academic Press, 2014.

LEGAL WRITING

Beazley, Mary Beth, *A Practical Guide to Appellate Advocacy*, Aspen Publishers Inc., U.S., 2006.

Entrikin, J. Lyn and Mary B. Trevor, eds. *Legal Writing Sourcebook,* American Bar Association, 2020.

McMurtry-Chubb, Teri A., *Legal Writing in the Disciplines: A Guide to Legal Writing Mastery*, Carolina Academic Press, 2012.

Tiscione, Kristin Konrad, *Rhetoric for Legal Writing: The Theory and Practice of Analysis and Persuasion*, West Academic Publishing, 2016.

PROFESSIONAL DEVELOPMENT

Abrams, Lisa, J.D., *Official Guide to Legal Specialties*, Gilbert, 1999.

Dunnewold, Mary L., Beth A. Honetschlager, and Brenda L. Tofte, *Judicial Clerkships, A Practical Guide*, Carolina Academic Press, 2010.

Maggio, Rosalie, *How to Say it*, Prentice Hall Press, 2009.

Rath, Tom, *StrengthsFinder*, Gallup Press, 2007.

ARTICLES

"About the American Legal Profession," britannica.com/topic/legal-profession

Culver, Leslie P., "Conscious Identity Performance," 55 *San Diego Law Review*, 577 (2018).

Culver, Leslie P., "The Rise of Self Sidelining," 29 *Women's Rights Law Reporter*, 173 (2018).

Fink, Jessica, "Gender Sidelining and the Problem of Unactionable Discrimination," 29 *Stanford Law & Policy Review*, 57 (2018).

"From Visible Invisibility to Visibly Successful: Success Strategies for Law Firms and Women of Color in Law Firms," ABA Commission on Women in the Profession, (2008); americanbar.org/content/dam/aba/marketing/women/visibleinvisibility_vs.authcheckdam.pdf

Godsil, Rachel, et al., "The Science of Equality in Education: The Impact of Implicit Bias, Racial Anxiety, and Stereotype Threat on Student Outcomes," (Feb. 2017), perception.org/wp-content/uploads/2017/05/Science-of-Equality-Education.pdf

Godsil, Rachel, "Breaking the Cycle: Implicit Bias, Racial Anxiety, and Stereotype Threat" (2015); nysba.org

Graham, Laura, "Why-Rac? Revisiting the Traditional Paradigm for Writing About Legal Analysis," 63 *Kansas Law Review*, 681 (2015).

Stras, David, Diane S. Sykes, and James A. Wynn Jr., "Panel Discussion: Judge's Perspectives on Law Clerk Hiring, Utilization, and Influence," 98 *Marquette Law Review*, 441 (2014).

Pollman, Terrill, "Building A Tower of Babel or Building a Discipline? Talking About Legal Writing," 85 *Marquette Law Review*, 887, (2002).

Tellez, Darhiana Mateo, "Clerkship Confidential: Judges Reveal What it Takes to Get Inside Their Courtroom," *ABA Student Lawyer* (March 2015).

WEBSITES

ABA 2020 Profile of the Legal Profession, americanbar.org/news/reporter_resources/profile-of-profession/

The Girl's Guide to Law School, thegirlsguidetolawschool.com

Imposter Phenomenon, paulineroseclance.com/impostor_phenomenon.html

Kirwan Institute for the Study of Race and Ethnicity, kirwaninstitute.osu.edu

Law Nerds: Skill building and advice about law school, lawnerds.com

Law School Admission Council, lsac.org

Learn How to Navigate Learning Disabilities in Law School, usnews.com/education/blogs/law-admissions-lowdown/articles/2017-04-03/learn-how-to-navigate-learning-disabilities-in-law-school

National Conference of Bar Examiners, ncbex.org

Perception Institute (studying explicit and implicit bias, racial anxiety, stereotype threat), perception.org

Project Implicit (Implicit bias association test-IAT), implicit.harvard.edu/implicit/takeatest.html

GLOSSARY

Accreditation The recognition by an official authorization, that a school has sufficient academic standards to qualify graduates for higher education or for professional licensing.

Advocacy The act of assisting, defending, pleading, or prosecuting a cause for another. The term "advocate" comes from the Latin term *advocare*, which means to "add" a "voice."

Altruistic Being mindful of others; having regard to the well-being or best interests of others; opposed to egotism.

Alumnus A former student of an educational institution. Most colleges or universities have alumni organizations whose members are actively engaged in a number of school-related activities.

Appellate advocacy The term "appellate" relates to an appeal, as when a client wants a decision of a lower (or trial) court to be reviewed by a higher court. That higher court is called an appellate court. Appellate advocacy is when a lawyer represents a client before a court that hears appeals.

Attorney A person who practices law; a lawyer.

Bar The whole body of lawyers qualified to practice in a given court or jurisdiction; the legal profession.

Bar association A professional association of licensed lawyers/barristers, where membership is based on commonalities such as region, ethnicity, or practice area.

Bar exam A written test that a person must pass before being licensed to practice law.

Barrister A lawyer who specializes in advocacy and litigation.

Bias The preference of one thing over another. It can be either positive or negative. In relationships, however, any tendency to believe that certain social groups are better than others can result in some people being treated unfairly.

Burnout A state of emotional, mental, and often physical exhaustion brought on by prolonged or repeated stress.

Campus The grounds and buildings of a school, college, or university.

Career fair An event that brings together employers and students with the purpose of establishing professional relationships and discussing potential job opportunities.

Case law The law to be found in the collection of reported judicial opinions that form all, or part, of the body of law within a particular jurisdiction. Case law is often referred to as the "common law."

Citation A technical requirement to support (or give proof of) a given interpretation of the law with legal authority or sources.

Civil system One of two major aspects of the legal system that concerns suits based in private rights. In a civil system, the plaintiff is either seeking a money judgment or equitable relief, such as an injunction or contract rescission.

Cocurricular Programs, activities, and events that supplement or enhance the broader learning and educational experience and that are not part of the academic curriculum.

Cohort Member of a similar group of people (such as students) who begin an educational program together, often take some courses together, and graduate in the same term and year.

Counsel Refers to the services provided by a person who legally practices law. This can also include a person who is retained exclusively by a company.

Criminal system One of two major aspects of the legal system that concerns public administration of penal justice, through which a person accused of a crime passes until the accusations have been disposed of or the assessed punishment is concluded.

Curriculum The subjects or classes comprising a course of study in a school or college.

Curriculum vitae A long-form resume that is usually submitted for positions in research and academia; abbreviated to c.v.

Dean The top or executive leader of a specific area of a college, university, or private school; has primary management and leadership responsibility for their unit.

Defendant A person accused in either a civil or criminal proceeding. Regardless of whether the proceeding is civil or criminal, the defendant is in the position of responding to accusations or allegations brought by a private party or the "people" of the relevant society.

Elective(s) Optional courses that students may select from a list of alternatives, that are designed to enhance the students' primary educational program.

Equity The intentional process or approach by which an organization provides access to the same opportunities to all of its members regardless of race, age, gender, or any other criteria.

Ethics A set of principles of right conduct. In law school having a good work ethic means that you place great value on hard work and diligence in doing good work.

Externship A university directed program that allows students to work for school credit. In law school, internship and externship are not interchangeable. Usually, internships are paid or volunteer positions, whereas externships are confirmed through the university and are considered a course of study. See also, Internship.

Faculty The body of teaching and, sometimes, administrative staff at a school, college, or university.

Fellowship A short-term position usually sponsored through universities, companies, or organizations and generally focused on the public service. Fellowships are paid positions and can last from a few months to a few years.

Grade point average Commonly referred to as GPA, this is a measure of a student's academic performance at an educational institution; calculated by dividing the total number of grade points received by the total number attempted.

Inclusivity An approach in which a person feels valued or welcomed in an organization. Inclusion has to be intentional, as it is not a natural byproduct of visible diversity.

Informational interview The first step in seeking a better understanding of a specific practice area.

Injunction A court order commanding or preventing an action.

Internship A paid or volunteer position where a student has the opportunity to gain practical legal skills. See also, Externship.

Jurisdiction A geographic area within which political or judicial authority may be exercised.

Legalese "Lawyerly" language that sounds stuffy (for example, "heretofore"). Also known as "legal jargon."

Legal concentration A grouping of related courses that allows a student to obtain focused knowledge and skill in a legal practice area.

Legal memorandum A written document used to inform the intended audience about the law, predict the outcome, and determine next steps.

Litigation The process of carrying on a lawsuit or the lawsuit itself. While the parties may settle a lawsuit before trial, the dispute always has the potential of ending in court for a trial.

Mentee A student who is trained or counseled by a mentor. Though the mentor is the more senior in relation to experience, the mentee is also responsible for contributing to the relationships through consistent communication and feedback.

Mentor A person who has expertise in a specific field, who serves as a role model and trusted source for information and guidance for a mentee.

Mock interview A practice interview. Mock interviews are a very important step in the pre-interview process, as they provide training on answering questions, body language, tone, and other areas of improvement.

Motion A type of legal writing that is persuasively written to the court to ask it to "move" toward a specific resolution for the client—for example, to obtain an asked-for order, ruling, or direction.

Networking The act of meeting professionals in various settings for the purpose of creating professional connections, learning more about a practice area, and discussing job opportunities.

Open note/book If a law school exam is designated open book or open note, then students are permitted to use their class notes or other study aids during the exam.

Persuasive writing The type of legal writing used when one represents and argues a specific side before a court for a resolution that favors their client.

Plaintiff The party who brings a civil suit in a court of law to remedy some harm done to them, that is not classified as a crime.

Practicum A course that includes an experiential component where students are supervised in the practical application of a theoretical course.

Predictive writing Writing in which one tries to predict, based on research, how a court might resolve a legal issue for a client.

Pro bono Meaning "for the good," pro bono refers to free legal services provided by attorneys.

Registrar The office or person in a higher education institution, responsible for assisting students in scheduling their courses, maintaining academic records, and corresponding with employers, licensing agencies, and alumni for proof of academic standing, program completion, and honors or awards attained.

Resume A written document that details your work history, education, professional memberships and other professional experience as it relates to a position.

Semester Two halves of an academic year. While, originally, the semester was six months, today, it is shorter than six months, lasting between 14 and 16 weeks.

Seminar A course that has a heightened level of rigor designed for an intense exchange of ideas. These courses are usually conducted in a small group setting but can also be offered to large groups.

Socratic method, the A technique of philosophical discussion by which the discussion facilitator (professor) questions one or more followers, building on each answer with another question, especially an analogy incorporating the answer.

Statute A written law passed by a legislature on the state or federal level that applies to specific situations (for example, forbidding or permitting specific actions).

Transactional lawyer A lawyer who primarily advises clients on legal issues affecting business and commerce.

Undergraduate Students who have generally graduated from secondary school and are enrolled in their first college or university degree program, but have not yet graduated.

INDEX

ACKNOWLEDGMENTS

AUTHOR ACKOWLEDGMENTS

Jendayi's acknowledgments: I'd like to thank the publisher for giving me the opportunity to be a part of your law school journey. The knowledge and experience I share with you could not be possible without the many students I have had the privilege of working with during my 15 years in legal education. I would like to thank them for helping me become a better educator and administrator. Thank you to Leslie and Robin, my coauthors, whose wisdom and experiences poured into this work to enrich and strengthen it. I would also like to thank my husband, Darryl, for his generous support during the hours and days I spent working on this book. Finally, I'd like to thank my son Chris, whose own authorship inspired me to begin and finish this work and for reminding me that there is always more to be done. Thanks for your support and encouragement!

Leslie's acknowledgments: To my husband Carl, and daughters, Faith and Nia, thank you for always giving me the space to thrive; all I do is for you! To Teri, thank you for the opportunity. To Anna, thank you for the amazing edits that made my words sharper. And to my coauthors, Jendayi and Robin, what a joy to work with you both—may our collective thoughts change lives and the legal profession for the better.

Robin's acknowledgments: I would not be an author without the patience and love of my greatest supporter and best friend, Michael Apodaca. Michael, my deepest appreciation and love belongs to you. Michael Jr., Zoe, and Christian, you three are my joy. I will never forget the celebration we had after submitting my last chapter. Singing "Mommy wrote a book!" in the kitchen is my new favorite song. To my mother, Julie, and my Aunt Marge, the strength and intelligence encompassed in your genuine love motivated me to accomplish many things. Thank you for listening and for your sage advice. I will cherish you always. Tremonisha, Khalilah, Cita, Krystal, and Akita. I am blessed to be surrounded by such profound women. Thank you for sharing your lives and experiences with me. I am a better friend, sister, mother, and boss because of you. To my first real boss, Gary Greener. Thank you for taking a chance on a 22-year-old fresh from college. I learned so much from you and was able to cultivate a career that I love. Jendayi, Lisa, Abbie, and Kathleen. Thank you for inviting me on this journey. I loved every minute.

IMAGE CREDITS